D1573132

EXPERIMENTAL VISION

The Evolution of the Photogram since 1919

Essays by
Floris M. Neusüss
Thomas Barrow
Charles Hagen

Roberts Rinehart
Publishers
in association
with the Denver
Art Museum

Cover illustration:
László Moholy-Nagy,
Hand Photogram (detail),
c. 1925, gelatin silver print.
Los Angeles County
Museum of Art:
Ralph M. Parson Fund.

Illustration p. 6:
László Moholy-Nagy,
Untitled (detail),
c. 1939, photogram,
gelatin silver print.
Collection of Jerry and
Emily Spiegel.

Illustration p. 38:
Arthur Siegel,
Lucidagram (detail), 1970,
gelatin silver print.
Courtesy Simon Lowinsky
Gallery, New York.

Illustration p. 54:
Adam Fuss,
Language of Echoes (detail),
1987, photogram. Denver
Art Museum: Joyce R.
Strauss Fund.

This book is published in conjunction with an exhibition
organized by Ted Strauss exclusively for presentation at the Denver Art Museum
January 15–March 27, 1994

Copyright © 1994 Denver Art Museum
All rights reserved under International and Pan-American Copyright Conventions.
ISBN 1-879373-73-4
Library of Congress Catalog Card Number 93-61702

Published in the United States of America
by Roberts Rinehart Publishers
121 Second Avenue, Niwot, Colorado 80544

Published in Ireland, Great Britain, and Europe
by Roberts Rinehart Publishers
Main Street, Schull, West Cork
Republic of Ireland

Printed in the United States of America
Distributed in the United States and Canada
by Publishers Group West

Edited by Marlene Chambers and Steve Grinstead
Translated by Cozette Griffin-Kremer ("From Beyond Vision")
Designed by Karen Embertson Design: Karen Embertson and David Skolkin
Printed by Johnson Printing

740514

Experimental Vision marks the culmination of almost twenty photography exhibitions curated by Ted Strauss over the last six years. The museum has eagerly supported him in developing an exemplary exhibition program and building an important contemporary photography collection. The people of Colorado have responded enthusiastically with generous funding and gifts of art.

It has been our goal to bring to our audiences work that reflects the latest directions in photography as well as historically significant antecedents. In tracing the path of the photogram since its "invention" by Christian Schad in 1919, Experimental Vision does both.

We are indebted to the lenders who have allowed their works to be shown in our museum. To those who have helped fund this exhibition and book, we are especially grateful—the Rose and King Shwayder Fund, the National Endowment for the Arts, the Joyce R. Strauss Fund, and the citizens who support the Scientific and Cultural Facilities District.

Lewis Sharp
Director, Denver Art Museum

Over the past two years I have found myself on a roller coaster of emotions and experiences while putting together the museum's first in-depth look at the photogram—a little-known photographic process that bypasses the camera/lens. Though the technique dates from the time of the earliest photographic experiments, the photogram was "rediscovered" in our own century by artists looking for a means to express dadaist and surrealist ideas.

We have not attempted to include in our survey all those artists who have, over the intervening years, used the photogram at one time or another. But we have endeavored to show work by some of the medium's principal practitioners since 1919: the four major explorers working in Europe who "discovered" the possibilities of the technique, its development by artists who came in contact with Moholy-Nagy in the Chicago area during the late thirties and early forties, and the directions it has taken since then in the hands of contemporary artists, primarily Americans, working with new materials and equipment.

A project of this dimension has required the help of many people. I am especially indebted to Floris Neusüss, whose definitive work on the photogram has been available only to readers of German. His early enthusiasm for the project and continuing help in locating rare images have been invaluable, and we are fortunate to be able to include here his incisive analysis of the intellectual currents that shaped the photogram's development. Thomas Barrow, who is a working photographer, a graduate of the Institute of Design, and a professor of art at the University of New Mexico, has personal knowledge of the Chicago school and has taught some of the artists included here. He has provided an insightful text on the photographers who came directly under the influence of the New Bauhaus. And Charles Hagen, *New York Times* art critic, has given us the benefit of his extensive exposure to contemporary photography by explicating the work of a large and diverse group of more recent innovators in this medium.

The Denver Art Museum staff has been dependably supportive through all the ups and downs of the project. I am grateful to my colleagues in the contemporary department, who have all been generous with advice and praise: Dianne Vanderlip, curator; Deborah Jordy, associate curator; and Jane Fudge and Nancy Tieken. Many others have also worked hard to make the project a success: Jeremy Hillhouse, exhibition designer; Julia Shepherd of the education department; Marlene Chambers and Steve Grinstead, editors; L. Anthony Wright, registrar, and his assistant, Pamela Taylor; and Cynthia Nakamura of the photography department. I have also enjoyed the help of Tom Bamberger, Jim Cohan, Susan Davidson, Ann de Villepois, Antonio Homen, Arnold Lehman, Amy Lipton, Robert Pincus-Witten, Howard Reed, Brent Sikkema, Mark Smith, Dave Tippit, Elan Wingate, Steve Yates, and Virginia Zabriskie. My sincere thanks to these and countless others who have assisted me.

The exhibition could not have been assembled without the generosity of lenders who have cooperated in every way to make their collections available to a wider audience. They have my deep gratitude. Finally, my special thanks to the two persons whose support I depended on most throughout this enterprise. First, Lewis Sharp, Denver Art Museum director, whose encouragement never wavered, and second (though always first in my affections), my wife, Joyce, whose judicious advice and tolerant acceptance of my roller-coaster moods made the undertaking not only possible but enjoyable.

Ted Strauss
Adjunct Curator, Photography

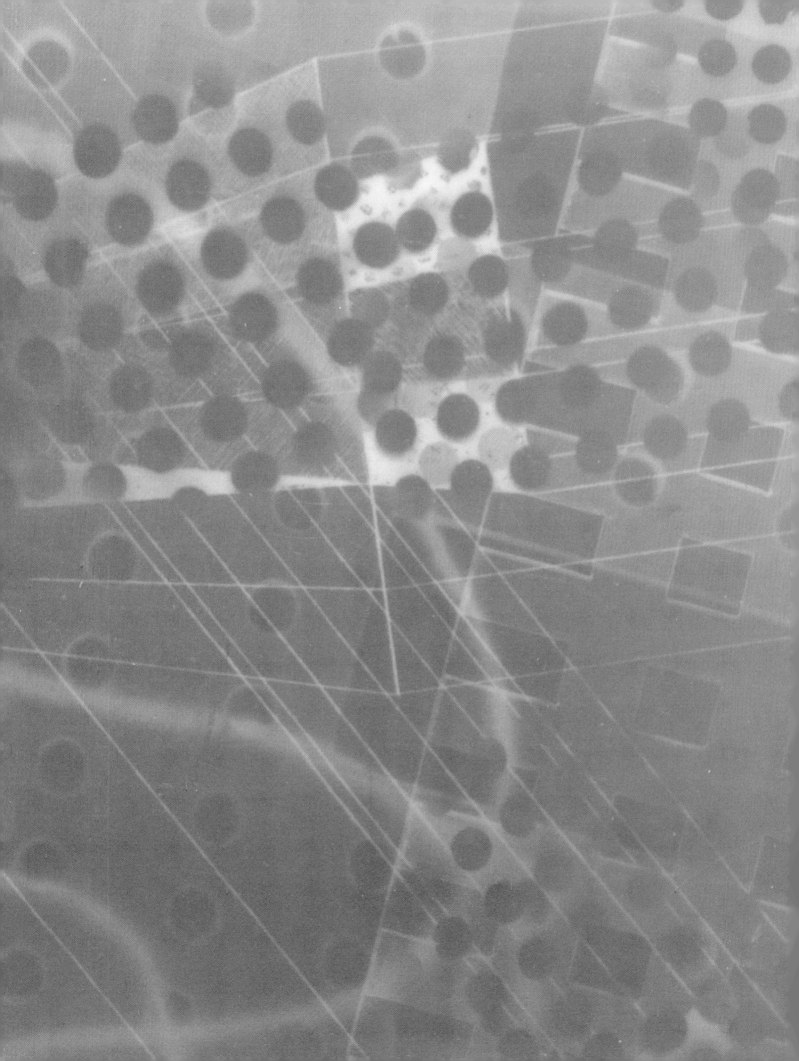

FROM BEYOND
VISION
Photograms by
Christian Schad,
Man Ray,
László
Moholy-Nagy,
Raoul
Hausmann

Floris M. Neusüss

The scientific debate that arose over the dimensions of space toward the middle of the nineteenth century began to penetrate the consciousness of artists by the beginning of the twentieth century. The old geometric orders had been enlarged by new, even contradictory geometries that could be applied to space. The collapse of old assumptions connected with a materialistically ordered way of looking at the world stimulated artists to use every possible means to explore this new space—space that could possess, as it were, an infinite number of dimensions. At the same time, a growing awareness of the limitations of human perception gave artists an added spur to try to grasp phenomena anew and to transplant them into a new ordering. Order itself came to be understood as a quality subject to constant transformation, one on which a lively mind could project itself. Those who took up this challenge suddenly saw the world with fresh eyes and were determined to submit everything to interrogation. Duchamp even suggested seeing three-dimensional bodies as the projection of four-dimensional constructs in the same way that we are used to seeing the projection of three-dimensional bodies in two dimensions.

Inventions, they say, are always made when they are needed. It is thus no accident that the photogram was invented at this time as a pictorial medium by artists who struck out into the new space to observe how everyday objects can transform their familiar qualities. In the photogram, objects turned into phenomena that otherwise do not appear to human perception. The artists who invented the photogram were fascinated by its almost automatic functioning, which somehow, though hardly in a definable way, obeyed the laws of optics. The process could be influenced at every point in its unfolding, but the results were unpredictable.

At this point, we must briefly outline what a photogram is technically and how it originated. If we define a photogram as a copying process whereby a stencil or an object is directly copied onto a photosensitive surface by light, we can interpret it very broadly. Understood in this way, a suntan that leaves the white pattern of a swimming suit on the body would be a photogram. The red apple with a yellow heart or star design that once delighted children might be called a photogram because the design was created by gluing a pattern on the apple before it ripened, thus blocking light to the design area. This kind of photogram occurs naturally, so to speak.

Photograms were made in the nineteenth century in connection with the invention of photography. Niépce, Bayard, Talbot, and others used them to test the light sensitivity of emulsions. Because the photogram (still without a name) could duplicate the most delicate structures with incomparable exactitude, it also began to be used in the natural sciences as a copying process for materials that would have been less precisely and more laboriously reproduced by drawings or photographs.[1] We could also count as a photogram the *cliché-verre*, in which a blackened glass

1. See, for example, Anna Atkins, *Photographs of the British Algae* (London, 1843).

plate with an etched drawing was copied onto photosensitive paper. In the nineteenth century, artists such as Corot and Delacroix used it to duplicate their drawings in a new way.

However, in the narrow sense, a photogram is a one-of-a-kind picture that occurs when photosensitive paper on which an object is laid is exposed to light and then developed. Since the twentieth-century artists who discovered this process for use in their work did not know about the history of the photogram in the nineteenth century, they can truly be called its inventors.

The accumulation of knowledge (quantum theory, relativity theory, atomic theory, etc.) at the beginning of the twentieth century led to a crisis in the sciences because these theories seemed suddenly to cast doubt on every certainty. This amounted to admitting that the only reliable statement that could be made was that objective knowledge was impossible for man because he was bound by his field of perception. Such humility contrasted starkly with the general euphoria about progress that pervaded public life. Most people believed that the problems of the future could be solved through the remarkable technical advances that were accumulating in rapid succession and increasingly influencing everyday life (electricity, air travel, railways, X-rays, movies, information technology).

Photography faithfully reflected these two polar attitudes. On the one hand, the self-congratulatory, self-confident way of looking at things yielded camera images that had come to be taken as "true," probably because they closely resembled human vision. On the other hand stood those painters, dilettantes in photography, who liberated it from the central perspective of the objective lens and "invented" the photogram while seeking iconographically neutral pictures for the mind's eye.

Between 1910 and 1920, sobered by the realization that human perception was imperfect and the sensations it created untrustworthy, artists looked for "objective" methods of representation. Because they felt that painting tends to communicate inner moods, they turned to "automatic" reproduction processes like photography or assembled pictures from "materials." Once they were no longer listening to their inner voices, they became aware of the expressiveness of the material itself and sought to allow its inherent liveliness and language to unfold in their work.

To throw more light on the context in which Christian Schad created the first photograms in art in 1919, we must also take into account the revolutionary influence of the dada movement. During World War I, Schad lived in Geneva and Zurich, the hub of the first dada movement, and was a close friend of Walter Serner, the extraordinary "fake" journalist, fake perpetrator of crimes, fake duelist, and language counterfeiter.[2]

2. Walter Serner, *Letzte Lockerung* (Hanover: Paul Stegemann Verlag, 1920).

As they watched the collapse of the belle époque from their Swiss refuge, the dadaists recycled its leftover rubbish to use as fertilizer for something new. Since the traditional view of the artist as inspired by "higher things" had also ended in the trash, Christian Schad took his inspiration from discarded fragments, worthless stray objects, and the microcosm of the wastebasket. In his tiny, jewellike photograms, this amorphous stuff, this hairball of civilization's flotsam and jetsam, shaped itself into noble groupings of fine figures, obviously in a state of grace and illumination. Schad gave some of them wonderfully senseless titles, like *Onéirodynie en Kova*. Sometimes he reworked the rectangular form of the photo paper with his scissors and even created new spaces by cutting small holes that look like stigmata.

His photograms were dadaistic in two senses: they were anti-art in that they adopted neither the means nor the subjects of traditional art, and they were anti-photography because they scoffed at the recognizable images of photography. Walter Serner understood this the instant he saw the little icons (approx. 25 pieces) and reported it immediately to the second dada headquarters that Tristan Tzara had set up meanwhile in Paris. Tzara, who had asked for material for a new issue of *Dada* magazine, thus published the first photogram in the history of art in *Dadaphone* in 1920 (although it was not called a photogram since there was still no name for this "new" process). It was also Tzara who later coined the term *schadography*, a pun that links the name of the inventor to the shadowlike character of the pictures.[3] After 1920 Christian Schad turned to realistic painting but once more took up the photogram technique in 1960, when he created over 180 images inspired by the nineteenth-century romantic prose poems of Aloysius Bertrand.[4]

The next inventor of the photogram was Man Ray, also a painter. Without much exaggeration, we might say that the thinking of Marcel Duchamp found its poetic-sensual expression in Man Ray's work rather than in Duchamp's own pictorial inventions, which, in a manner of speaking, bypass the retina and aim directly for the cerebral. At the very beginning of their friendship in New York (1915), Man Ray benefited immensely from Duchamp's skepticism in his own search for ways to leave behind the world of the given and the obvious. The American adopted the European's mistrust of the emotional values of painting and sought out techniques that bore no signature. He happened on the airbrush technique first. In a process very like the photogram, he created white forms on a color background by placing objects on white paper and spraying them with paint.

Man Ray's actual "invention" of the photogram in 1922, shortly after his move to Paris, may have occurred either by accident or through Tzara, who may well have shown him Schad's photograms. The fact that Man Ray himself later portrayed his invention as an unconscious, "automatic" happening in the darkroom[5] places it in the context of the "automatic writing" (*écriture automatique*) of his surrealist colleagues André Breton and Philippe Soupault. This relationship had already been suggested by the title Man Ray chose for his 1922 photogram album, *Champs délicieux*,[6] which echoes the title of a 1919 book of automatic writing by Breton and Soupault, *Les Champs magnétiques*. In fact, the photograms in *Champs délicieux* look like representations of the word clusters in *Les Champs magnétiques*. Man Ray has quite ordinary, everyday objects, many of which we recognize, pop up in his *Champs délicieux*. They hover around there like suddenly freed, living beings that had been shut up for ages and, unobserved in the shelter of darkness, were taking their first steps in the cosmos.

They must have made this impression on Man Ray's friends, who were the first to see the pictures, for in his preface to *Champs délicieux* Tristan Tzara marvelously acknowledged the enrichment of vision that Man Ray's photograms achieved. Entitling his text "La Photographie à l'envers" (Photography Inside-Out), he poetically portrayed the confusion that had overtaken an "art grown arthritic" in the face of "great inventions and stormy weather," by which he meant those scientific discoveries that required a new conception of objects and space. He scorned the "subtle brushwork" of traditional painting: "Originally this slight quivering was a weakness that called itself sensitivity in order to legitimize itself. Human imperfection does seem to have more worthy merits than the precision of machines." He went on to render homage to Man Ray, the

3. Tristan Tzara, cited by Georges Hugnet in *Fantastic Art, Dada, Surrealism*, exhib. cat., ed. Alfred H. Barr, Jr. (New York: Museum of Modern Art, 1936), 276.

4. Aloysius Bertrand, *Gaspard de la nuit: Fantaisies à la manière de Rembrandt et de Callot* (Paris: Pincebourde, 1842). Schad had access only to the 1928 Paris edition published in the Scripta manent series.

5. Man Ray, *Self Portrait* (1963; reprint, New York: MacGraw-Hill, 1979), 128-29.

6. *Champs délicieux*, album with twelve rayograms and a Preface by Tristan Tzara (Paris, 1922). The title makes a rhyming pun on Paris's famous Champs Elysées.

"dealer in light values," for these totally new pictures that seem almost to create themselves, "as a mirror effortlessly reflects an image, or an echo the voice, without asking why." Furthermore, they are of an entirely different and more suitable nature than painting, Tzara noted, for they are "physical-chemical products."

As Man Ray himself said, things could become objects of affection for him. His photograms give the impression of an almost erotic relationship fully unfolding in the very distance that the automatic picture process places between the artist and his "models." Whether the models for his photograms were objects, plants, or his friend Kiki, we always have the impression of witnessing a situation of intimacy between him and them. The fact that the object touches the photographic paper during exposure but is gone in the image reveals an essential characteristic of the photogram —a sort of absence is felt as a presence in these pictures.

Man Ray linked his "invention" immediately with his own name. As early as 1922, he was calling these photographic pictures "rayographs."[7]

In the glass cases of the Poincaré Institute in Paris, there were (and still are) dusty figures that look like little sculptures. Someone from the surrealist circle discovered them by accident, and these "mathematical objects," each incarnating a particular conception of space (whether Euclidian or non-Euclidian), landed in the 1936 exhibit of surrealistic objects at the Ratton Gallery after being photographed by Man Ray.[8] As the surrealists had recognized immediately, the models owed their existence to the will to transcend defined space that we also feel in the artistically effective works of sculptors. This will is communicated in a poetic way in Man Ray's photographs of these objects, and we find it again in his photograms, a good many of which give the impression of being "mathematical objects" because they arise out of the laws of what Paul Eluard called the "physics of poetry" *(illus. p. 24).*

The study of moving bodies also belongs to the field of physics, and the study of bodies in light was one of the tasks that twentieth-century artists set themselves again and again. We have Man Ray to thank for a dadaist-kinetic experience in what appears to be the only photogram movie in film and art history. *Retour à la raison* (The Return to Reason) was shown in 1923 at the last dada soirée, "Le Coeur à barbe" (The Bearded Heart). The idea for the film was simple and ingenious: Man Ray cut unexposed movie film into long strips, nailed them on a table lengthwise, sprinkled them with pepper, salt, needles, thumbtacks, strands of wool, and so on, exposed them, and developed the pieces. Afterwards, he glued them together in alternation with realistic footage. The projection set the thumbtacks into wild, dancing motion.

The third painter to invent the photogram, shortly after Man Ray in the fall of 1922, was László Moholy-Nagy, who was living in Berlin at the time. He, too, was seeking an automatic process that would produce pictures without transferring expressive values through the hand and brush. He believed that, because brush techniques too easily express sentimental values, they negatively affect the purity of a picture as a spiritual product for spiritual use. In his search for a neutral process, he went so far as to order three pictures in enamel technique from a sign maker by telephone.[9]

He soon concentrated on light as a medium that could paint itself. In his youth, Moholy had already developed an almost ecstatic relationship to light, which he conceived of as energy in

7. The first use of the term occurs in *Little Review* 9, no. 3 (1922): after p. 16 on unnumbered pages.

8. Twelve of these photographs appeared with an essay by André Breton, "Crise de l'objet," *Cahiers d'art* 11, nos. 1-2 (1936).

9. Floris M. Neusüss, *Das Fotogramm in der Kunst des 20. Jahrhunderts* (Cologne: DuMont, 1990), 110-11.

motion. As a constructivist painter, he had attempted to depict light and space in a dynamic relationship of forces in movement. Photography revealed to him, however, a process by which light could, unassisted, etch itself on photosensitive surfaces. The only thing that interfered with this direct link between light and the photographic surface was the lens, and Moholy's "invention" of the photogram consisted in taking the lens out of the photographic process, thus allowing light to represent itself as a living, material precipitation: he had finally succeeded in replacing the pigment of painting with light.[10]

In giving his new technique the name *photogram*, Moholy emphasized its immediacy by analogy to the rapid and direct communication of impulses by telegram.[11] The cosmic, almost colorless spatial effects he had sought to achieve in his paintings through heightened constructs of transparent, dematerialized forms were arrived at in the photogram even more convincingly and, as it were, automatically—without showing a trace of the hand. The loss of color in the photogram was more than made up for by an unlimited spectrum of greys.

His photograms seemed all the more lifelike in comparison to the paintings that preceded them, which sometimes gave the impression of being too "theoretical." In his first photograms, he used geometric and rather two-dimensional elements that harked back to his paintings *(illus. p. 26)*, but he soon began to use three-dimensional objects as light modulators. In these photograms, we perceive light as a flowing, space-creating matter constantly transforming itself and suggesting the flow of time, with its potential to change the physical shape of objects.

In order to achieve such effects and avoid adding a narrative element, Moholy obviously had to prevent the objects he used to modulate light from being recognized. Exceptions to this were flowers *(illus. p. 30)*, his own and his wife's head, and his hand *(illus. p. 27)*. Time and light bring flowers out in the photogram as well as in nature; the hand is the hand of the painter who lets light paint, who makes light phenomena "graspable," who acts to shape and change, and who sees himself in constant change, as his portrait shows *(illus. p. 31)*.

New scientific concepts—Albert Einstein lived and worked in Berlin and had described the world as a four-dimensional space-time continuum—influenced conversation in Berlin artists' studios where, along with all kinds of competing philosophies, they had a many-sided effect on artistic production. The predominant attitude in Berlin avant-garde circles was a rejection of sense perception as the basis for artistic statement and a determination to escape from the confinement of its physical cage. Artists endeavored to orient experience toward something beyond three-dimensional space (naturally, there were all sorts of mystical and occult speculations going about), and they could clearly no longer accept a finite, immutable standpoint for observing the world.

Every relation can also be defined by the inversion of its values. The reaction of photographic emulsion to light, the "light paradox," represents this sort of inversion of values because light darkens the photographic layer. What shine out as bright in photograms are precisely the areas that are not struck by light. When Moholy re-inverted the tones of a photogram for this very reason, he provided a picture of the "relativity of experience" *(illus. pp. 28 and 29)*.

In 1930, he completed a self-moving sculpture that transformed the light hitting it into thousands of moving light and shadow pictures. This kinetic sculpture, referred to as the Light-Space Modulator or Light Requisite, was composed of metal shapes made of transparent, opaque, and

10. Moholy discussed his photogram idea for the first time in "Produktion - Reproduktion," *De Stijl* 7 (July 1922): 97-101, and later in "Light: A Medium of Plastic Expression," *Broom* 4, no. 4 (March 1923): 283-84, where his photograms were first published.

11. Moholy introduced the term *photogram* in his *Malerei Fotografie Film* (Munich, 1925), Bauhaus Book no. 8.

12. Moholy published the conception of the Light-Space Modulator in *Die Form*, nos. 11-12 (1930): 297-99. The machine was included in the *Werkbund* exhibit in Paris, 1930.

13. László Moholy-Nagy, "Fotogramm und Grenzgebiete" (Photogram and Borderlines), *i 10* 3, nos. 21-22 (1929): 190-92.

varyingly reflective materials that had no formal value on their own but were meant to catch light and transform it into changing, virtual pictures.[12] Thus, it was something more than a machine to make pictures; it was an object that demonstrated a harmoniously functioning form of consciousness open to transformation and creating transformation itself.

As early as 1929, Moholy had imagined that "light studios should take the place of the outdated painters' academies."[13] He was able to apply this idea later in his own school, the Chicago "New Bauhaus," where work in the light laboratory was a standard part of the curriculum.

Even in this last stage of his creative life, light remained the most important energy for him, though his work took another new turn. He took up painting again and also created sculptural objects, often of plexiglass and sometimes in conjunction with paintings. However, photograms continued to play an important role in his repertory.

The most recent of his photograms included here *(illus. p. 33)* displays a dimension he had previously excluded from his work. Being in America seems to have helped him finally overcome the often doctrinaire demands for exclusion of all personal values from art works, particularly as these were articulated in Berlin by the Russian materialists, who, following Lenin, still believed in "eternal verities" rooted in the immutability of matter. Although Moholy's principle of "value inversion" denied materialism by pointing up the relativity of experience, he had, for altogether different reasons than the materialists, sought to avoid self-expression in his art. Still, his later American works benefit from his taking the liberty to express in them the personal, unconscious, and intuitive values he felt were connected with "biological laws." Although we can see his 1939 photogram simply as a construction of a soberly strict spatiality, an amorphous, meandering, soft line adds those "biological-organic" qualities that make it potentially inhabitable.

Raoul Hausmann arrived in Berlin in 1900 as a fourteen-year-old and lived there until 1933. Hence, he grew up as an artist at a time when Berlin and Paris were the two European hubs of the international avant-garde. As a self-taught artist, he had absorbed extensive scientific, philosophical, and literary knowledge, especially in the theory of perception, and by 1912 he was writing on every imaginable theme. In contrast to most of his fellow artists in Berlin, who felt obligated to define their philosophical positions in opposition to some line or another, Hausmann adopted the principle of not excluding anything but of letting as many contemporary threads of thought as possible influence his own ideas and art.

This attitude of setting no limits on the possible also applied to his choice of artistic media and extended to the use of his body in dance as an organic medium of expression that could grasp and shape space and time. In his "sound poems," he let his voice make up a language composed only of sounds without meaning. The pictorial counterpart of these sound poems were his "billboard poems" with giant, arbitrarily juxtaposed letters. These poems had what Hausmann called an "opto-phonetic" effect because they were pictures meant to be seen *and* heard. We can truly say that Hausmann was a practicing theorist of perception.

The Berlin dada phenomenon lasted from about 1918 to 1921, and Hausmann was on the "board of directors" of the group. The infantile, onomatopoeic term *dada* described the dadaists' childlike way of coming to terms with phenomena—taking things apart and putting them back together anew. Although Hausmann never essentially changed his way of working, he later transformed the disruptive dimension of dada ideas into a more constructive, almost didactic element.

The 1920s, when he was shaping his artistic identity, were shadowed by the memory of World War I, while the political situation again grew more acute during the 1930s. Convinced that the inflexibility of human perception was the root cause of human catastrophes, Hausmann undertook a lifelong study of the preconceptions and consequences of perception and sought to communicate his findings in his work, which included extensive texts. He saw photography as an outgrowth of the same general precipitousness that shaped urban life and criticized it as an instrument that limited human perception. From this criticism, he developed a theory of photography that provided an essential contribution to the discussions about photography in the Berlin of the 1920s.

In 1918, Hausmann had invented the "photomontage," in which photographs, often torn from newspapers, commercial brochures, and other printed matter, were allowed to interact turbulently with other pictorial elements and especially with speech material. In this way, he forced on photography what he found lacking in it—vision taking place at several levels, at different times, with references to as many influences as possible. Proceeding from this standard, his credo so to speak, he finally began making photographs himself, just a few at first in 1926, and then increasingly after about 1930. Of course, he was familiar with the photograms of Moholy-Nagy and Man Ray, and even on friendly terms with Moholy-Nagy, but photograms did not attract his interest until much later. However, he did make a series of photographs in 1930 that prefigured his photograms to a certain extent. At the same time that Moholy-Nagy was working with his Light-Space Modulator, Hausmann was also attempting to come to terms with light (in a somewhat more down-to-earth way than Moholy-Nagy) and photographed a light-space environment he had constructed with a chair, a light bulb, and a few pieces of white paper. In these photographs, which he later called "melanographs" (from the Greek, *melanos*, for black), he can be said to have introduced a third quality alongside light and shadow—nonlight.[14] In a figurative sense, the rays of nonlight can be equated with the unknown, which for Hausmann was the companion of all phenomena. In the photogram, the paradoxical picture par excellence, nonlight—the area where an object entirely protects the photographic surface from exposure to light—is converted into the purest brightness, beaming out like the light of knowledge. Beside this is the shadow thrown by the object and the areas of deepest blackness, where the photosensitive paper was struck by light unhindered by any obstacle.

Hausmann called the photogram a "technical form similar to abstract painting that belongs only conditionally to the field of photographic vision."[15] As a process similar to collage, it was an ideal technique for him, an artist continually endeavoring to see or put phenomena in new relations. After a wartime odyssey that led him over half of Europe, he settled in Limoges in 1944 and took up the photogram in 1946 as part of his repertory. He used it in entirely new connections by making it a functional element of his personal time curve; that is, he linked it either to moments from the past or to the present action that was being imprinted on the photogram. He incorporated it into distinctive collages, in which he fused torn photos, drawings, gouaches, etc., from various periods of his work to make an entirely new, wholly individual time map. In the collage included here *(illus. p. 34)*, a 1948 photogram is used as the background for torn photos from

14. Hausmann's two texts on melanography appeared in *Camera* 20, no. 12 (1942): 301-2 and 311, and in the album *Melanographie*, 61 copies (Paris: Edition SIC, 1968).

15. Hausmann, unpublished manuscript, uncatalogued collection of Hausmann papers, Marthe Prévot, Limoges, France.

16. On the photopic-
togram, see Neusüss, *Das
Fotogramm in der Kunst des
20. Jahrhunderts*, 330-31.

1931 Berlin and 1947 Limoges. In other photograms *(e.g., see p. 36)*, his action of moving torn or recut papers between successive exposures remains present in the picture as space-creating time layers. In this way the artist himself is actually present in the picture along with the light and the material.

We can observe this in its ultimate concentration of content and form in Hausmann's *photo-pictogram* series,[16] consisting of some fifteen items, one of which appears here *(illus. p. 37)*. The only material Hausmann used in these photograms was sawdust. He scattered it on photographic paper, wrote signs in it with his finger, and then exposed it.

In spite of their visual parsimony, these photopictograms blend many of the artistic forms of expression that Hausmann had forged in the course of his life and which, like his collages, keep these periods alive. Here we have a thread running between *dance*, the *billboard poems*, the *sound poems*, and the *vision poems* (the written signs of the photopictograms refer to language, but language freed from meaning, reduced to sound and communication), as well as the *photograms*, the *collages*, and the *melanographs*. As in the melanographs, the forms in the photopictograms are neither positive nor negative, or even both at once. The sawdust, the only material he uses that leaves visible forms behind, operates as if it were an idea of matter instead of a substance. Visible forms or nonforms are also left by Hausmann's action—the writing of signs. Those signs are references to a movement of the mind. In his photopictograms, Hausmann brought together in one picture the most polar extremes imaginable—matter and spirit—as "harmonious contradiction."

Not too long ago, matter and spirit were still understood as irreconcilable opposites, as the very principle of separation and differentiation. The surrealists had already run up against this and sought a synthesis of matter and spirit in the union of opposites. Man Ray's photograms can be seen in this light. Moholy-Nagy and Hausmann also found in the photogram a pictorial form that reflected their individual conceptions of this opposition between forces. As a spiritual materialist, Moholy-Nagy attempted to bring polar forces into harmony, and Raoul Hausmann let the vibrant conflict between matter and spirit, this "harmonious contradiction" that he sought elsewhere than in equilibrium, operate as a driving force to provide the energy of life.

Modern science has denied the duality of matter and spirit. This promises a fortunate dissolution of binary systems of thought in favor of a new diversity that may even be determined by chaos and the new orders formed from it. It appears that the elimination of the comfortable matter/spirit opposition has succeeded in undermining polar standpoints in art and created a new perplexity that often has a crippling effect. Perhaps we can see here and there (quite certainly in Sigmar Polke's work) the first pictures in which this challenge operates as a driving force.

From top:

Untitled Schadograph
1919
2³⁄₈ x 2²⁵⁄₃₂ in.

Schadograph
1919
3¹⁄₈ x 2³⁄₈ in.

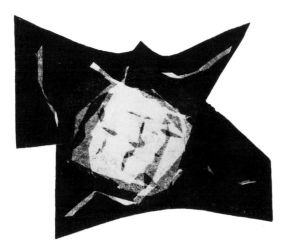

From top:

Amourette
1919
2½ x 3½ in.

Renseignements
1919
2⁵⁄₁₆ x 3⁵⁄₁₆ in.

Transmission
Ischiatique
1919
2³⁄₈ x 3¼ in.

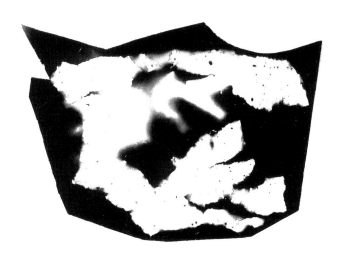

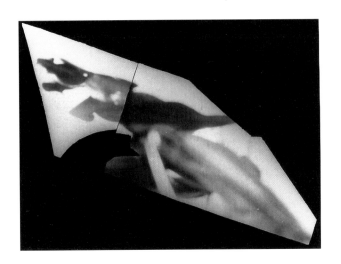

MAN RAY

Untitled (Rayograph)
1922
11 $^7/_{16}$ x 9 $^5/_{16}$ in.

MAN RAY

Untitled (Rayograph)
1923
9⁷⁄₁₆ x 7⅛ in.

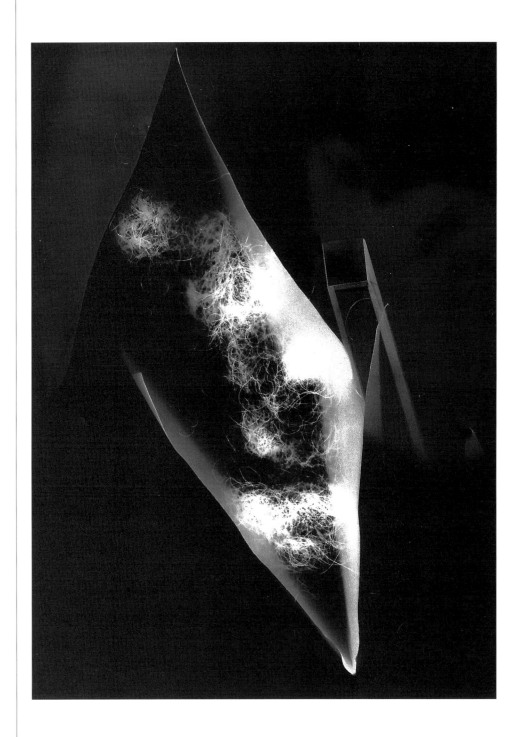

*Gun with Alphabet
Squares*
1924
11⅝ x 9¼ in.

MAN RAY

Sugar Loaves
1925
$9^{3/16}$ x $11^{5/8}$ in.

**LASZLO
MOHOLY-NAGY**

Untitled
1922
3¹/₂ x 5¹/₂ in.

Hand Photogram
c. 1925
9 ³/₈ x 7 ¹/₁₆ in.

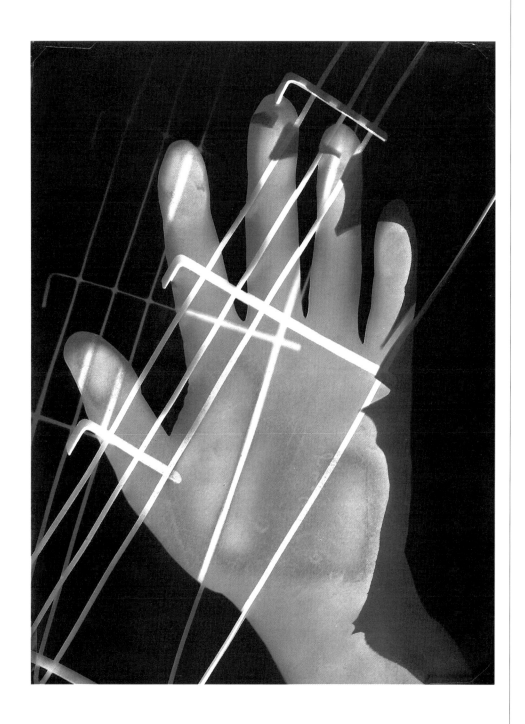

Untitled (Goerz)
1925
11⅞ x 8⅞ in.

Untitled (Goerz)
1925
11⅞ x 8⅞ in.

**LASZLO
MOHOLY-NAGY**

Blumenfotogramm
1925
9⁵⁄₁₆ x 7 in.

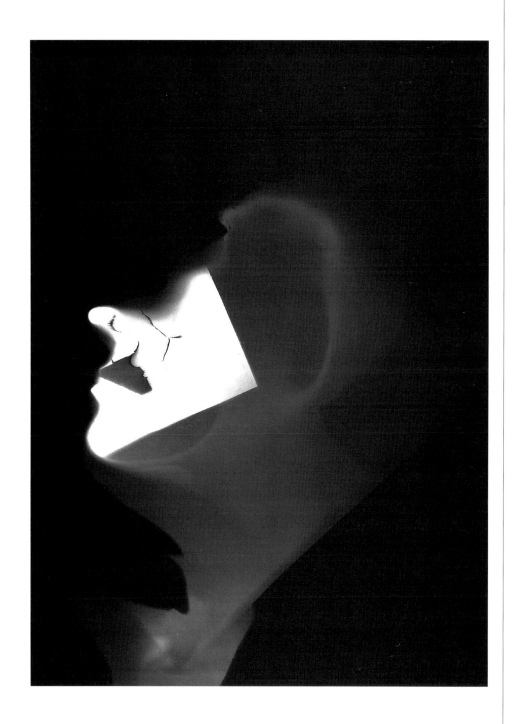

Untitled
1925
7⅛ x 9⁷⁄₁₆ in.

Untitled
1948
13¾ x 11 in.

Untitled
1950
13⅞ x 11¼ in.

Untitled
1954
15⁵⁄₁₆ x 11⁷⁄₈ in.

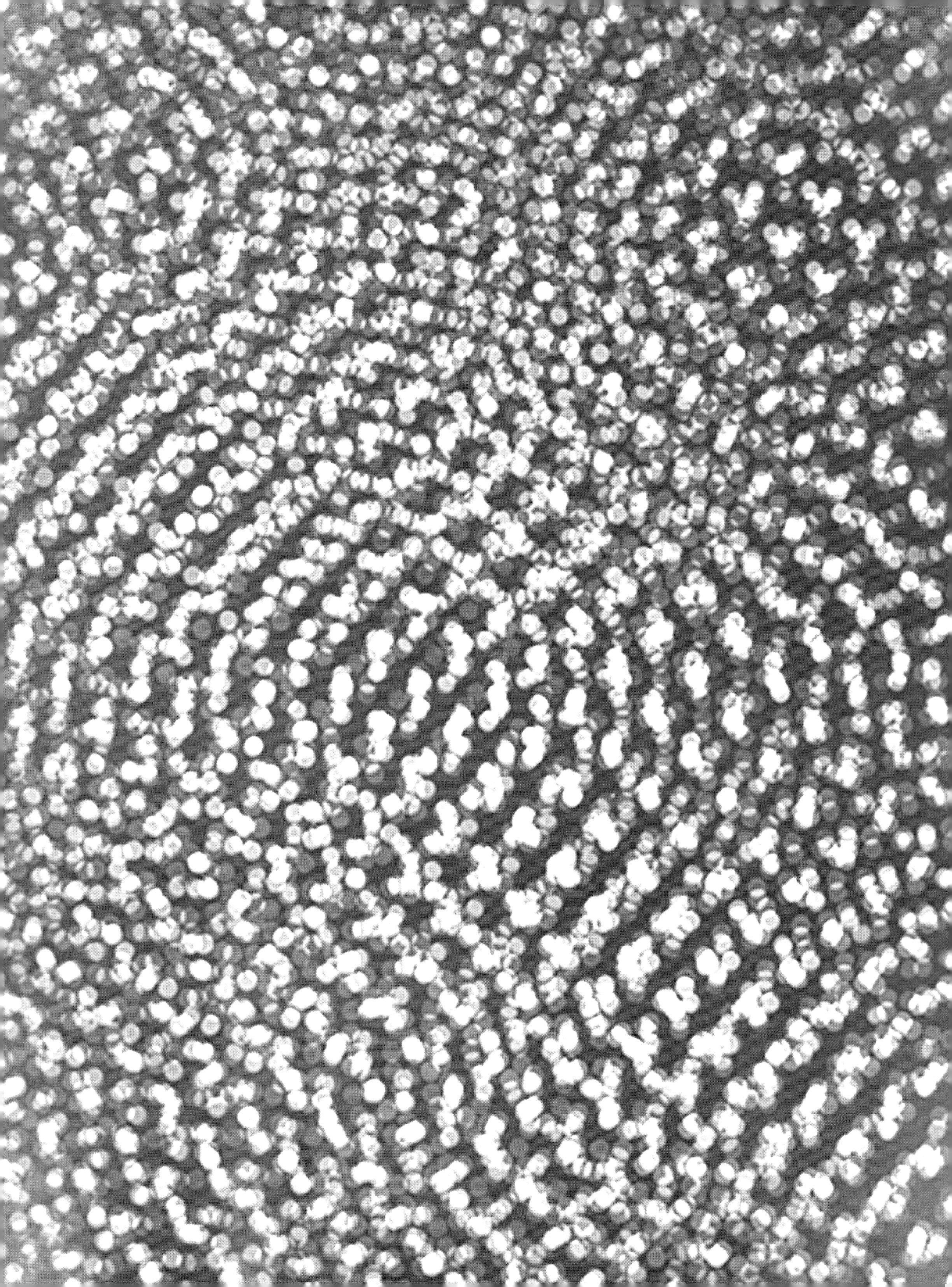

Thomas Barrow

The origin of the photogram in the United States is vague and poorly documented, but any discussion of the discovery and use of the photogram must begin with László Moholy-Nagy and the New Bauhaus in Chicago. The story of how Moholy-Nagy came to Chicago has appeared in numerous publications, but, since most of these sources are out of print, a brief recapitulation is appropriate. Moholy-Nagy was already well known in European art circles by the time changes in the school's administration provoked his resignation from the Dessau Bauhaus in 1928. During the next eight years he traveled and exhibited widely, temporarily settling in London in 1935. In 1937, at the suggestion of Walter Gropius (who had come to the United States at the beginning of that year), he applied for the directorship of a school that was to be known as the New Bauhaus in Chicago, founded by the Association of Arts and Industries. Within a year, financial difficulties forced the school to close, but with the help of Walter Paepcke, the far-sighted president of the Container Corporation of America, Moholy-Nagy was able to keep the School of Design he opened in 1938 afloat until it was finally incorporated into the Illinois Institute of Technology as the Institute of Design in 1944. During his first three years in Chicago an extraordinary range of artists encountered Moholy-Nagy. What many of these artists took away from these meetings was not his philosophy of painting, although he always preferred to be thought of as a painter, but his utopian, modernist ideas about light and photography.

These ideas encompassed several media and were clearly intended to upset the status quo. In brief, they declared that merely imitating nature was archaic and no longer served modern sensibilities, which were being altered by the increasing political tensions in Europe that followed World War I. The idea of revolution was part of this atmosphere and was implicit in much avant-garde writing about art. Moholy-Nagy's writings were no exception, and he viewed photography as a key component of the sweeping changes he was proposing for vision and for life itself. He was, however, somewhat inconsistent in his theorizing. He extolled the camera, for instance, in a frequently quoted phrase that predicted that ignorance of this device would define the illiterate of the future. At the same time, he saw the elimination of camera apparatus when making the photogram as symbolic of the liberation that could come from total abstraction. In fact, he viewed the photogram as a profound reordering of space-time and a significant revolutionary act.

Several of the photographers represented here met Moholy-Nagy upon his arrival in Chicago and are now associated with what is sometimes called the Chicago Bauhaus.[1] Gyorgy Kepes, Arthur Siegel, and Henry Holmes Smith were all at the New Bauhaus from the beginning: Siegel as a student and Kepes as head of the Light Workshop with Smith assisting in photography and managing the photographic darkrooms. Shortly before Moholy-Nagy's death in 1946, Siegel was

1. The following sources have been consulted for information regarding the New Bauhaus and the early years of the Institute of Design: Andreas Haus, *Moholy-Nagy: Photographs and Photograms*, trans. Frederic Samson (New York: Pantheon Books, 1980); Richard Kostelanetz, ed., *Moholy-Nagy* (New York: Praeger, 1970); Charles Traub, ed., "The New Vision: Forty Years of Photography at the Institute of Design," *Aperture* 87 (1982).

appointed head of photography. Theodore Roszak's connections to Moholy-Nagy began in 1930 when Roszak was in Munich and acquired a copy of *Malerei Fotografie Film*, the 1925 Bauhaus book that constitutes the first of Moholy-Nagy's major theoretical works. In it he states that he "seek[s] to identify the ambiguities of present-day optical creation."[2] Roszak finally met Moholy-Nagy when he came to New York City as a consultant for the Design Laboratory, a WPA-funded school where Roszak was teaching. Their friendship began at this time, and it is clear from their correspondence that Roszak showed Moholy-Nagy examples of his photograms in the mid 1940s.[3]

Whatever commonality the works included in this book might share beyond the process itself is probably most obvious in their lack of overt content. There is nothing in the way photograms are made that precludes content, and much of the work that was created apart from Moholy-Nagy's teaching explored the possibilities of metaphorical and allegorical themes. Man Ray's large body of work in this form is the most often cited; however, the photograms of the Czech photographers Miroslav Hák and Hugo Táborský and early work by Jaromír Funke indicate that they could infuse their photograms with deeper meaning.[4]

There are many areas in Moholy-Nagy's use of photography where human emotion and meaning are a part of the finished work. The photomontages *Jealousy, Structure of the World*, and *The Shooting Gallery* are frequently reproduced examples. The fact that references to human foibles, Darwinian incongruities, and man's inhumanity to man never appear in his photograms is a clue about the way he viewed the process in his overall theoretical scheme and, by extension, the kind of influence he exerted on those who came under his teaching at the Chicago Bauhaus. It is clear from his writings on photography that the photogram was a primal form, the Ur photographic source. In the essay "A New Instrument of Vision," he states,

> The photogram, or camera-less record of forms produced by light, which embodies the unique nature of the photographic process, is the real key to photography. It allows us to capture the patterned interplay of light on a sheet of sensitized paper without recourse to any apparatus. The photogram opens up perspectives of a hitherto wholly unknown morphosis governed by optical laws peculiar to itself. It is the most completely dematerialized medium which the new vision commands.[5]

The way this passage prefigures Clement Greenberg's dicta regarding painting's autonomy and an unswerving truth to the medium is one indication of the range and depth of Moholy-Nagy's theoretical speculations. It, along with much of his writing, has the polemic tone of the avant-garde and makes it easier to comprehend why many of his students appear to have followed his lead slavishly.

As suggested above, Moholy-Nagy acted in a variety of ways as a mentor to each of these photographers, but he may have had the least visible impression on Arthur Siegel. Since his death in 1978, Siegel's reputation has been enhanced by his early photograms and his connection with the New Bauhaus, but little attention has been given to his long career as a photojournalist and architectural photographer, one that reveals an extremely competent professional with few traces of his close early ties to Moholy-Nagy's teachings. While most of Siegel's photograms from the late 1930s and 1940s, before he entered the Air Corps, bear the stamp of the master, they do not reveal any particular inventiveness or enthusiasm to extend the formal possibilities of the process.[6]

2. László Moholy-Nagy, *Painting Photography Film*, trans. Janet Seligman (Cambridge, Mass.: MIT Press, 1969), 7.

3. Beth Urdang, *Photograms* (New York: Zabriskie Editions, 1984), 8.

4. Jaroslav Andél, et al., *Czech Modernism: 1900-1945* (Boston: Bulfinch Press, 1989).

5. Moholy-Nagy, "A New Instrument of Vision," *Telehor* (Brno, 1936); reprinted in Kostelanetz, *Moholy-Nagy*, 50.

6. A number of Siegel's surviving photograms are undated, but they are believed to date from his brief tenure as a student at the New Bauhaus, where they would have been made under Moholy-Nagy's supervision.

The photograms he made after returning to the Institute of Design in 1946 are of greater variety. Some of them suggest an awareness of the cut-paper photographs of Francis Bruguière and also serve to remind us that Siegel was extremely well read in the history of photography. In the late 1960s he sometimes gave a class at the Institute of Design in the history of the medium from a Freudian viewpoint, while simultaneously urging his students toward greater experimentation and discovery in their visual work. It is, at least in part, in the wide-ranging interests of Siegel and his attraction to photojournalism that one finds connections to the ideas that were manifest in the teachings of the New Bauhaus. The widely reproduced 1941 image, *The Right of Assembly*, possesses the same roiling energy seen in photographs from Russia at the time of the revolution. There is no disputing the fact that the photographic vision of the Bauhaus informed a part of Siegel's entire body of work, but the photogram was a small portion of that body; and for Siegel it simply could not contain the greater message he sought to convey.

Because Henry Holmes Smith and Arthur Siegel were at the New Bauhaus at the same time, one is tempted to find similarities in their work and lives, and in fact there are a number. Obviously, both worked with the photogram, and photojournalism and commercial work also played a part in their individual careers. But perhaps most significant was the deep commitment each had to education. Siegel commented, "What I am proudest of in my life is not my photography, but my educational contribution."[7] Smith's pedagogical commitment was as great as Siegel's, and, while he wrote a great deal about the early years at the institute and Moholy-Nagy's influence, he was also clear about his own philosophy:

> I went to considerable lengths to try to find out what would strengthen each one of those students as a person. . . . And some of them recognize it and acknowledge it; some of them don't and that's fate. But when you do that, you don't wind up with homogenization, you don't wind up necessarily atomizing the people either. They grow around their own center. And that's the one place where I would have disagreed ultimately . . . with Moholy. I think the individual's more important than the culture in a culture like ours.[8]

The preceding discussion and quotations begin to suggest the intellectually and idealistically charged atmosphere that surrounded these photographic adventurers. For our own revisionist time this atmosphere has often been criticized as pedantic, soulless, and—the ultimate condemnation—elitist. Most of the detractors have not looked very carefully at the great beauty the best photograms distill from pure light, nor have they thought very deeply about the nonobjective theory connected with this process. Max Kozloff, a critic who has written widely on photography, described most cogently what he perceives as the photogram's tragic flaws:

> [V]ery little was made visible in photograms. Being the reverse of normal photography, in that they revealed only what obstructed the light, not what was illuminated by means of it, photograms were very limited in their resources. . . . Moholy lacked the irreverent fantasy of Man Ray and that talent for the fastidious recycling of urban chaff that distinguished his friend Kurt Schwitters. . . . In this self-contained art form, the illusive dimensions of photography are made as shallow as the symbolic resonance of the motifs is thinned out. . . . Moholy's photograms have so far failed to extend out of their compromises into the culture of later generations.[9]

These rather harsh, yet astute observations lose some of their strength as one reads on to find that

7. Arthur Siegel, quoted in Traub, 35.

8. Henry Holmes Smith, quoted in Howard Bossen, *Henry Holmes Smith: Man of Light* (Ann Arbor: UMI Research Press, 1983), 132.

9. Max Kozloff, *Photography and Fascination* (Danbury, N.H.: Addison House, 1979), 127-29.

they serve to prove that the "zenith" of Moholy-Nagy's art was in his naturalistic photographs. While the flaws Kozloff points to may be seen as inherent, a less prejudiced approach might have revealed how the photogram's apparent negation of linear perspective freed photography from the literal depiction of nature and how the making of prints without mechanical apparatus anticipated aspects of process art and minimalism.

The problems of critical acceptance faced by the photogram parallel those of concrete poetry and other formal experiments in literature when they were compared to more traditional narrative structures. The avant-garde in literature and the profound influence of T.S. Eliot, Ezra Pound, and James Joyce are extraordinarily well documented, but when the concept of the avant-garde is placed in the context of photography, it remains problematic for many critics. Richard Kostelanetz, a critic and cultural historian, believes:

> One explanation for why avant-garde works should be initially hard to comprehend is not that they are intrinsically inscrutable or hermetic but that they challenge the perceptual procedures of artistically educated people; it is their nature to forbid easy access or easy acceptance.[10]

The issues of acceptance were inextricable from the making of photograms for the artists identified with the New Bauhaus. They were always implicit in Henry Holmes Smith's lectures and his numerous essays.

> [Photographers] could study the new art for structures that were adaptable to traditional photography and incorporate these into photographs made directly from nature. Or, by one of several combinations of photographic and non-photographic techniques, they could create a synthetic imagery (more photo-pictures than photographs) quite close in spirit to the new art, but a whole world away from traditional photography.[11]

While all of the polemic surrounding the making of photograms suggests a humorless intensity in these artists' endeavors, it is not the whole story. Smith's work often contains a barely concealed wit in references to the fluidity of the Karo syrup he used as a drawing element for his photograms, as well as in his titles for the abstract figuration of the prints *The Alchemist, Diver and Fish*, and *Grotesque*, among others.

Although the pedagogical and aesthetic positions of the New Bauhaus photographers are of considerable interest to the serious viewer, one can turn to the work of Theodore Roszak with a certain relief. His images are relatively unencumbered by "position papers" of any kind: for Roszak "the machine was a tool, not an ideological entity."[12] In almost all of the extant photograms by him there is a sense of how exciting it was to create a trace with pure light and the quotidian object. Many of them resemble studies for his constructivist sculptures and later biomorphic constructions, yet they always convey a much greater sense of transparency than any of the reliefs or freestanding pieces.

Roszak appears to have made no photograms after 1941, and it is interesting to speculate on the reasons for this. It may be, as gallery director Beth Urdang thinks, that the "intimacy of the darkroom was an anathema during the war, when artist's [*sic*] studios already seemed excessively indulgent havens."[13] A political motivation seems less likely than the possibility that Roszak, who was primarily a sculptor as well as a dedicated modernist, found the paper-based photogram too ephemeral. He could not create the streamlined illusions in two dimensions that were so

10. Richard Kostelanetz, *The Avant-Garde Tradition in Literature* (Buffalo, N.Y.: Prometheus Books, 1982), 4.

11. Smith, quoted in *Aaron Siskind: Photographer*, ed. Nathan Lyons (Rochester, N.Y.: George Eastman House, 1965), 17.

12. Theodore Roszak, quoted in Joan Marter and Michael Zakian, "Photograms by Theodore Roszak: In Light of the Bauhaus," *Arts* (Nov. 1984): 122.

13. Urdang, 10.

convincing in the *Bi-Polar* constructions. He nevertheless created in a very short period of time a body of photograms that may be seen as quintessentially modern, an almost textbook assimilation of Moholy-Nagy's theories.

Of these four Chicago Bauhaus artists, the one with the closest ties to Moholy-Nagy was Gyorgy Kepes. A Hungarian like Moholy-Nagy, he was eleven years younger and greatly impressed by his countryman's early work and teachings. He moved to Berlin in 1930 to work with him and expand his experimentation in still photography. Joining Moholy-Nagy at the New Bauhaus in 1937, he left in 1943 to finish work on *Language of Vision*, published the following year. In many ways this publication was an expansion and refinement of Bauhaus teaching methodology and its basic philosophy. At the same time, it was the most thorough outline of the new vision's utopian grand scheme to save mankind. As S.I. Hayakawa writes in the book's introductory essay:

> The reorganization of our visual habits so that we perceive not isolated "things" in "space," but structure, order, and the relatedness of events in space-time, is perhaps the most profound kind of revolution—a revolution that is long overdue not only in art, but in all our experience.[14]

Much of this visionary discourse was shaped by technology and its discoveries. These, of course, included photography, and Kepes and Moholy-Nagy made frequent reference to it. In our age, with its ever-increasing numbers of the technophobic, the optimistic text may appear misguided, but it is easier to understand when we learn Moholy-Nagy stated that he never saw a machine until he was a grown man,[15] with the implication that, when he did, he and those around him were changed forever.

Kepes's book has been reprinted many times and has had a wide-ranging influence on artists and designers in the United States. It was the impressive first of many published works by Kepes and remains one of the best sources for a complete understanding of how these artists thought about photography's role in changing the world. Toward the end of the book, under the subheading "Disintegration of the fixed system of meaning organization," Kepes describes photography's contribution:

> [E]ach photograph carried within itself characteristics of the world from which it was taken. The observer was forced to find order in the unrelated fragments, to trace back some latent meaningful connections in the basically meaningless haphazard . . . collages or photomontages. The wider apart the elements were in meaning and the more impossible it seemed to find integration for them, the greater became the tension of the spectator as he struggled to find a source of integration. This tension was a zero point of the meaning organization. It served as a basis for redirection.[16]

Kepes's own photograms illustrate much of what the sometimes convoluted prose is struggling to say. He incorporated the widest possible variety of materials to exploit the negative appearance that is commonly associated with the photogram. He also utilized film negatives to create positive/negative tensions in his images. As he enlarged upon his early influences, he became more and more convinced of the inherent value of what could be learned from structures found in the natural world. Interestingly, this view seems to converge with those espoused by the architect and theoretician Buckminster Fuller. In a 1984 conversation with Diana du Pont, Kepes summarized

14. S.I. Hayakawa, "The Revision of Vision," in Gyorgy Kepes, *Language of Vision* (Chicago: Paul Theobald, 1944), 10.

15. John Anthony Thwaites, "Perhaps the Best Verdict," *Art and Artists* (Apr. 1975): 29-30.

16. Gyorgy Kepes, *Language of Vision*, 205.

his way of working as the bringing together of

> a staccato, fragmented light space with some more structured rhythmic pattern of geometric shapes. This juxtaposition or opposition of the free undisciplined and the geometrical disciplined is a persisting motive in my work.[17]

There really has not been any end to the photographic issues raised by these disparate, yet often like-minded artists. Much of their work was provoked by the limitation of the photograph articulated in 1934 by Bertolt Brecht in the tenth anniversary issue of *Arbeiter Illustrierte Zeitung*:

> The tremendous development of photojournalism has contributed practically nothing to the revelation of the truth about the conditions in this world. On the contrary . . . the vast amount of pictured material that is being disgorged daily by the press and that seems to have the character of truth serves in reality only to obscure the facts. The camera is just as capable of lying as the typewriter.[18]

Once the sociopolitical nature of work made at this time has been acknowledged, the documentary nature of photograms becomes obvious. They are as representative of national concerns and humanistic ideals as any Farm Security Administration photographs. It was, to a great extent, the unrealized dream of these artists that the nonrepresentational photogram would convey as much feeling and information as the most detailed photographic record of everyday life.

In the final analysis, it was Moholy-Nagy who held the greatest hope for what the photographic process in the hands of artists might bring to mankind. Today, when artists have become as cynical as politicians, his dreams are in danger of appearing merely quaint; but, in looking at his images and those of artists he influenced at the Chicago Bauhaus, one can still sense their optimism. In his final, posthumously published manifesto, *Vision in Motion*, Moholy-Nagy called for a "Parliament of Social Design" that

> could serve as the intellectual trustee of a new age in finding *a new unity of purpose*. . . . It could write a new charter of human life, culminating in the right to *and the capacity of* self-expression . . . without censorship or economic pressure.
>
> It could translate Utopia into action.[19]

17. Kepes, quoted in Van Deren Coke with Diana C. du Pont, *Photography: A Facet of Modernism* (New York: Hudson Hills Press in association with San Francisco Museum of Modern Art, 1986), 58.

18. Bertolt Brecht, quoted in Douglas Kahn, *John Heartfield: Art and Mass Media* (New York: Tanam Press, 1985), 64.

19. Moholy-Nagy, *Vision in Motion* (Chicago: Paul Theobald, 1947), 361.

ARTHUR SIEGEL

Lucidagram
1970
17 x 14 in.

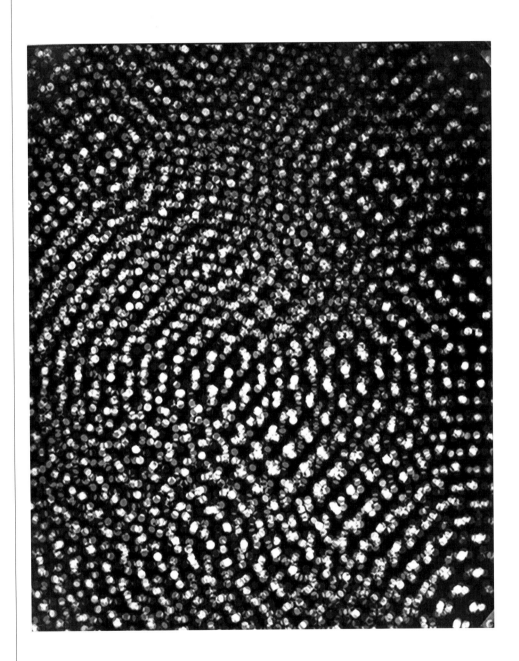

Lucidagram
c. 1970
14 x 17 in.

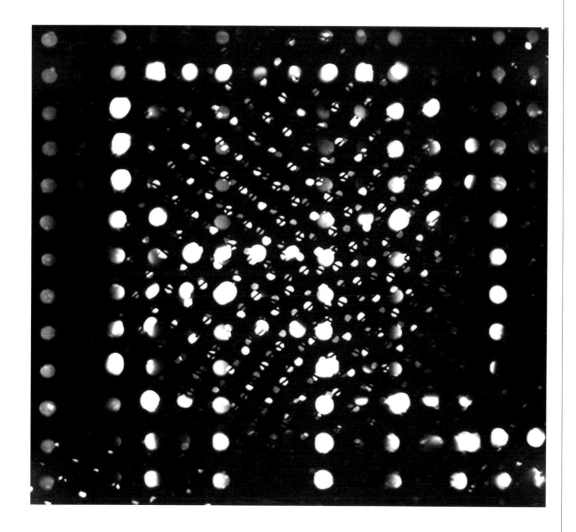

Untitled
c. 1937-39
11 $^{7}\!/_{16}$ x 8 $^{7}\!/_{8}$ in.

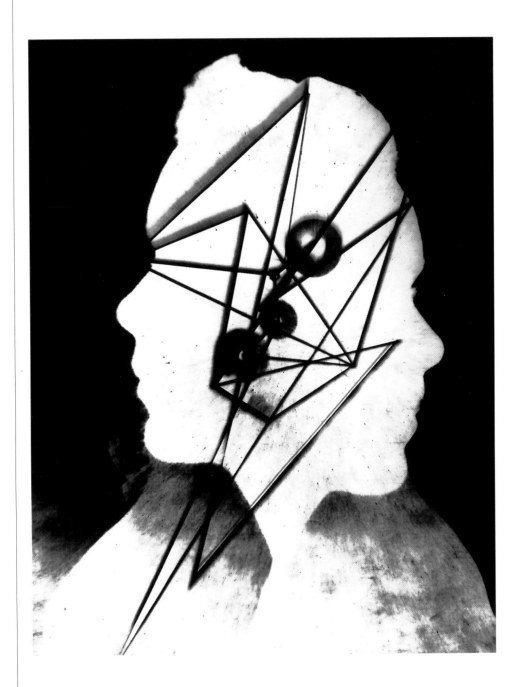

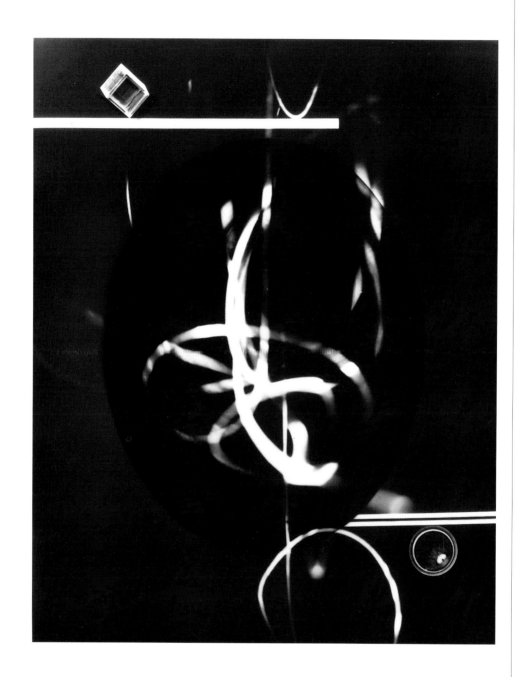

THEODORE ROSZAK

Untitled
1937-41
4¾ x 4 in.

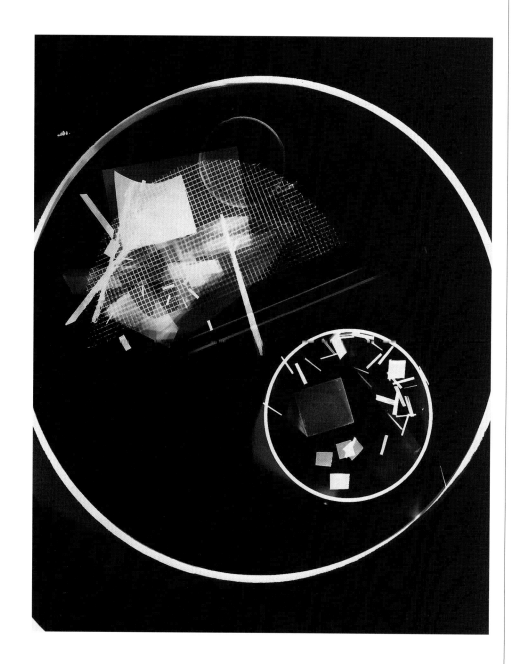

**HENRY HOLMES
SMITH**

*#3 Refraction
Drawing*
c. 1949
13⅞ x 10⅞ in.

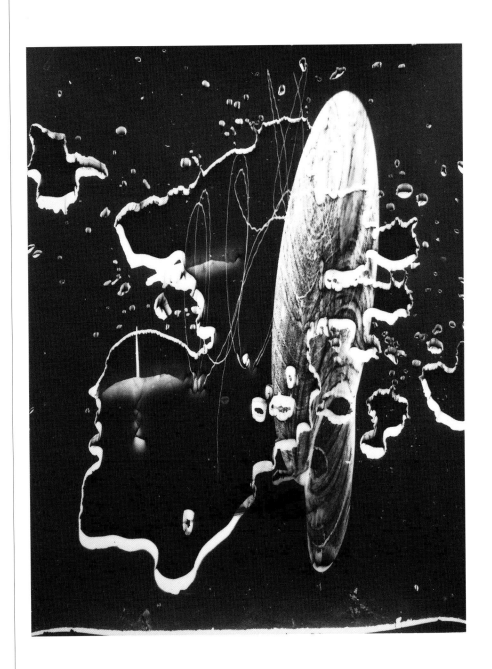

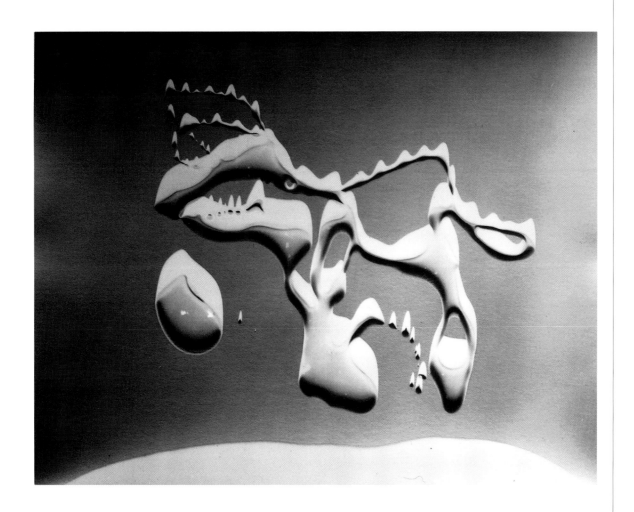

Charles Hagen

The history of photograms has remained largely hidden, a constant but little noticed undercurrent in the broad stream of photography. In part this may result from the reluctance of critics, curators, and even photographers to accept photograms as an intrinsic part of the medium. Emotionally as much as physically, these shadowy, allusive images seem the reverse of the forthright, declarative pictures produced by conventional photography. Photograms are like photography's bad twin, the dark side of the nineteenth-century faith in description that is implicit in the medium.

Photograms have rich psychological implications. They offer artists and viewers alike a sense of anarchic freedom, of the conscious mind gone on holiday. Made without the intervention of a lens, which maps the objects of a scene in mathematically regular relationships produced by Renaissance perspective, photograms seem to capture a primal photographic quality. Like fish that live in the deepest parts of the ocean, the strange and beautiful forms found in photograms appear to have eluded the logical net with which perspective ensnares the world of things.

In their depiction of the world, photograms seem cruder and yet more honest than conventional photographs. In a photogram the shapes of objects are impressed by light onto the surface of chemically sensitized paper; the resulting images are the exact size and shape of the objects that produced them. However strange and limited they may seem, photograms provide a more immediate, and even more accurate, form of depiction than images produced by the camera and lens. Like X-rays, photograms reveal unexpected aspects of reality.

Many artists in this century have been attracted to photograms. During the 1920s, surrealists like Man Ray and constructivists like László Moholy-Nagy found in photograms a tool with which to express their different artistic visions. Both these artists tried to push photography beyond its traditional task of recording the face of the material world in conventional terms, and photograms offered both a door to another reality.

In recent years a wide range of artists have produced photograms, sometimes as a major strain of their work, sometimes as a central concern. A primary source of photograms' current appeal is the widespread interest among artists in allowing chance to dictate the form of art works or in using processes with little conscious manipulation to produce unforeseen results.

This tendency involves a change in the conception of the artist's role and the nature of artistic activity. Rather than being something like a self-conscious craftsperson who shapes an image or object according to a predetermined set of aesthetic criteria, the artist becomes a kind of aesthetic scientist experimenting with a wide variety of materials and processes in order to see what happens. The results are judged not solely as an expression of cultural fashions and tastes, but as revealing the aesthetic dimension of the physical world. Working in this way, artists hope to escape from their prejudices and training, which have become suspect as reflecting personal and cultural biases.

This impulse toward spontaneity, widespread in contemporary art, is related to dadaists' efforts in the early decades of the century to enlist chance in creating art works. Paul Klee created collages by dropping bits of colored paper onto a background sheet and pasting them where they happened to land; Marcel Duchamp dropped lengths of thread onto the ground and then cut templates out of wood to match the curves they formed.

The interest in chance and process was continued by the abstract expressionists, who explored the effects of various ways of applying paint and who often used wax, bits of fabric, and other materials in their works. A similar direction can be found in contemporary painting, where artists have begun to reinvestigate different paint applications and the expressive possibilities of drips, stains, and puddling.

In the 1960s many conceptual artists carried on this interest in the workings of process and chance. Such artists as Sol LeWitt, John Baldessari, Vito Acconci, and Douglas Huebler produced work not according to their own aesthetic decisions, but based on logical or mathematical systems. The work they created in this way seemed to be the product not of the artist's will, but of the world itself.

The belief that the unmediated processes of nature could themselves be an important means of making art was anticipated by some of the earliest descriptions of photography. When William Henry Fox Talbot, the English gentleman who invented the first paper-based photographic process, presented his pictures to the Royal Institution in London in January 1839, he described a photogenic drawing of his estate that he had made four years earlier as "the first instance on record of a house having painted its own portrait."

For many conceptualists of the 1960s and 1970s, photographs served as an apparently neutral way of documenting the results of their experiments as well as providing a kind of surrogate found object, in effect bringing the world into the gallery. The thrust of much of the work done by these artists and their many successors today has been to observe and analyze the world rather than to create an image of it. Photograms, whose mysterious and evocative images seem even closer than lens-based photographs to the essence of the world, have provided these and other artists with a powerful image-making tool.

Robert Rauschenberg

The three small blueprints by Robert Rauschenberg illustrated here *(pp. 63-64)* have seldom been seen, let alone exhibited, since their creation in 1951. They are among approximately thirteen such prints that Rauschenberg and his then-wife, Susan Weil, made as miniature versions of the full-scale blueprint works they were producing at the time.

In the *Print Collector's Newsletter* (September/October 1993), Mark Smith reports that Rauschenberg and Weil photographed ten of the larger blueprint pieces, using film internegatives, and made the smaller prints on commercial-grade blueprint paper. The artists used these smaller prints as Christmas gifts and sent them as promotional pieces to art directors and others when they were seeking magazine assignments and work designing store windows.

All but one of the works are figurative; the subjects—Weil holding a cane, with her skirts around her like a fan, or a male figure in a dancelike pose with one leg and one arm cocked and the other arm outstretched—have both a compositional boldness and formal surprise. These silhouetted figures also continue the exploration of questions of transparency and light that can be found in Rauschenberg's photographs of the period as well as in his later prints and paintings.

Sigmar Polke

A leading figure in the revival of interest in German art, Sigmar Polke is best known for paintings, often on stitched-together pieces of fabric, in which he combines images from divergent sources. These works allude to subjects ranging from recent German history to alchemy. But Polke has also been an energetic and far-ranging photographer, exploring X-rays, multiple exposures, and multiple prints, as well as photograms, with exceptional freedom.

In both his paintings and his photographic work Polke has demonstrated his interest in processes and in the alchemical suggestions implicit in art making. In one series he incorporated such esoteric materials as meteorite dust and photosensitive silver compounds into varnishes which he then applied over wall-size canvases to produce works that have a ghostly power. His photograms, represented here by *Der Jungbrunnen*, 1984 *(illus. p. 77)*, are equally wide-ranging, incorporating bits of old prints, photographic reproductions of paintings, snapshots, and other elements into complex, allusive works.

Bruce Conner

The California artist Bruce Conner is best known for his drawings, collages, and films, including *A Movie* (1958), in which he spliced together snippets of newsreels and other found footage to create an ominous exploration of American life. Over the past two decades he has also made photograms by recording bodies lying on photographic paper *(see p. 68)*. The resulting blobby figures, life-sized, suggest the endoplasmic shapes of spirit photography.

A parallel to these full-scale figural photograms can be found in the *Anthropométries* made in the 1950s by the French artist Yves Klein. In these famous works Klein coated nude models with paint and then pulled them across the surface of canvases.

Other artists, notably Robert Rauschenberg and Floris Neusüss, have also made photograms of the body. For them, as for Conner, photograms have provided a way to take a direct and un-mediated imprint of reality.

Robert Heinecken

For more than thirty years the Los Angeles artist Robert Heinecken has deployed a knowing and sometimes sardonic wit and a sharp sense of formal exploration to examine the hidden subtext of popular culture from magazines to television to fast food. In his *Are You Rea?* series he exposed magazine pages on photographic paper to create new images that combine photographs and headlines on both sides of the printed pages *(illus. pp. 71 -72)*.

The surprising conjunctions of ads and articles that result seem absurd but often have a dream-like logic. In his *Food Polaroids*, Heinecken used a different but equally effective tactic, placing food directly on the photographic material to create mysterious and evocative images out of mundane materials *(illus. pp. 73-74)*. Combining elements of pop art, dada, and process art, Heinecken's deliberately provocative work has influenced a generation of younger photographers on the West Coast.

Frederick Sommer

Before he perfected his pioneering daguerreotype process, Louis Jacques Mandé Daguerre, the French painter and showman, experimented with a kind of picture he called *dessins fumées* (smoked drawings). He produced these odd works by "drawing" with the smoke of a candle onto drawings or engravings in order to create subtle chiaroscuro effects.

The results of Daguerre's experiments are unconvincing either as precursors of photography or as drawings, with soot in blotchy smudges covering sections of the underlying images. But in his 1963 work Frederick Sommer used a similar process to far greater effect, drawing an abstract form on glass to create a negative from which he produced the final print. Now eighty-seven years old, Sommer has long used unfamiliar photographic processes to create images that have surrealist overtones. Working with the gestural freedom of abstract expressionism, he produced in this piece *(illus. p. 65)* a billowing, plumelike tangle that suggests a labyrinth or a swirling cloud of force.

Gilbert and George

The English artists Gilbert and George first achieved fame in the 1960s with their performances as "singing sculptures." In this role they sang English music-hall ballads while standing on a table with their faces covered with silver paint, dressed as modern-day dandies in neat suits and ties. For more than twenty years, though, the two artists have created large, multipanel photographic works, many of which include images of themselves. Typically they appear in their dandy personas in situations that offer veiled narratives of their lives as artists. A common theme that runs through many of these works is their Englishness, with images of such national icons as the Houses of Parliament.

In *Raining Gin*, 1973 *(illus. p. 67)*, more than forty small pictures flow down the wall, each presenting an image of one or the other artist (actually cut-out sections from a joint portrait in which one sips from a wine glass). At the top of each image is a photogram of a glass. With its topsy-turvy form, the tumbling images of glasses overlaid on the staid portraits, and the reference in the title to gin, the quintessential upper-class English drink, the piece typifies the blend of formal adventurousness and autobiographical and social references that characterizes the pair's best work.

Lucas Samaras

Renowned for obsessively worked and elaborately patterned paintings, drawings, and sculptures that are often characterized by an interest in his own image, Lucas Samaras has also made important groups of photographs since the 1960s. These include an extensive series in which he altered SX-70 Polaroid pictures of himself by pushing and squeezing the dyes inside the prints to create often monstrous self-portraits. Using luridly colored lights and patterned cloths to provide garish visual backdrops, he later posed friends nude in his studio and photographed them with a large-format camera. Samaras himself appeared in each picture, usually in the corner, a demonic *magister ludi*.

In *Skull & Milky Way*, 1966 *(illus. p. 66)*, Samaras combines a central symbol of mortality with an image of infinity, the spangled night sky of the Milky Way. This riveting work suggests a cosmic X-ray made by the light of the stars themselves; in its overtones of death and spiritual transcendence it restates themes found in much of Samaras's work.

Barbara Kasten

Sculpture and the layering of space have been central concerns of Barbara Kasten's photographic works. Kasten's first photograms, produced in the late 1970s, formed a natural transition from the textile sculptures she was making at the time. In these early photograms *(illus. p. 75)*, Kasten coated sheets of paper with photosensitive emulsion and exposed them through sections of fiberglass window screening. By using two layers of screening at slightly different angles she could create moiré patterns; by adding inks to the emulsion she could produce large stains of color in different parts of the image.

Kasten thought of these works as related to Morris Louis's paintings made by dripping thinned-out acrylic paint down unprimed canvas. Later she incorporated the shapes of boxes and other objects in her photograms; it was not until 1979 or 1980 that she began to use a camera to make her pictures.

Today Kasten is known for lavish architectural photographs in which geometric shapes of color carve up the space of the picture. But her photographic work continues to reflect her background in sculpture and her attempts to find ways of creating space in her pictures.

Thomas Barrow

Joining image to image according to associations of subject and form, Thomas Barrow creates dense crazy quilts of reference in his photograms. In *Artificial Curiosities*, 1984 *(illus. p. 76)*, he combines decorative elements, including the lacelike filigree of wrought iron (taken from a pattern book), schematic trees of the sort used in architectural drawings (transferred from plastic sheets), a section of track from a model train, and patterns of stitchery.

To the photogram background of his piece Barrow has stapled a grid of Polaroids of toys. These objects bring a threatening note to the domestic theme of the work. A robot appears to glare out of one frame while a shogun doll looms ominously in another.

Barrow made the photograms in this series between 1978 and 1985. With its mix of the shadowy, negative forms of photograms and brightly colored, flash-lit Polaroids, *Artificial Curiosities* suggests a blend of the past and the present, public and private, explicit and hidden.

Elizabeth Bryant

In the Hispanic neighborhood of Los Angeles where Elizabeth Bryant lives many businesses use painted signs of objects—a loaf of bread for a bakery, an engine for a garage—as a way of dealing with the mix of languages residents speak. Bryant became intrigued with these signs and began to incorporate silhouettes of common objects like a cup, a house, or a key in her work. Later, trying to create combinations that had a formal unity rather than a direct connection, she began to stencil simplified renderings of other common objects onto these shapes.

In *Hand/Snake*, 1987 *(illus. p. 78)*, she incorporates images of things associated with hands, including scissors and a bracelet, into a large photogram of a hand; over this image she has stenciled an image of a snake. Other pairings from this series are equally unexpected and often surprisingly evocative: a photogram of a cup is combined with a stenciled image of a bird in flight, a photogram of a rose with the picture of a bed (making a punning reference to a rosebed), and a photogram of a flame with an image of hands making the string figure of a cat's cradle.

Adam Fuss

Adam Fuss's *Language of Echoes*, 1987 *(illus. p. 69)*, suggests a scientific illustration of the structure of an atom or the solar system. Fuss made the print by placing a piece of photographic paper in a tray of water and sprinkling water across the top to achieve an effect like that of throwing pebbles into a pond with concentric circles rippling across the surface and colliding with one another.

In a more recent work *(illus. p. 84)*, Fuss arranged the entrails of a rabbit in a decorative pattern on a large sheet of color photographic paper and then exposed them to light. In the resulting image the shapes of the intestines are like decorative scrolls of ribbon. Some of the strange colors of the images in this series are created by the light that is blocked or partially transmitted by the entrails. But the juices of the intestines have eaten into the photographic paper itself and produced a strange rainbow of acid reds, oranges, blues, and yellows.

James Welling

Strictly speaking, James Welling's *Degradé* images are not photograms at all. He placed no objects onto the sheet of photographic paper but instead simply exposed it to light under an enlarger and changed the color filtration during the exposure. In this way he created strangely evocative images that suggest at first blush the moody fields of color found in the works of such painters as Mark Rothko and Barnett Newman.

Like much of Welling's work, these images grew out of his interest in the conventions of commercial photography. (Welling worked for a time as a catalog photographer for an auction house.) In his best known work from the 1980s, Welling presented images of inconsequential items—for example, soap flakes that looked like chips of paint—against elegantly swagged black velvet curtains. In the images here *(illus. pp. 80-81)*, made in 1989, Welling re-created the gradated sheets of color used as backdrops in commercial photography; the title he gave all these works, *Degradé*, is the term used by studio photographers to describe these color backgrounds. As with his other pictures, Welling tried to reveal the industrial underpinnings of the romantic conventions of commercial photography and our culture in general.

Joseph Nechvatal

By replicating over and over drawings and images taken from popular media, Joseph Nechvatal produces dense, tangled patterns that are the visual equivalent of radio static or the background noise of an electronic system. Out of these cloudlike forms emerge the images themselves, like ghosts of intended messages that have been obscured by the means of transmission—the photographic process itself.

Nechvatal adds to the otherworldly, futuristic quality of these images by presenting them as paintings made with the Scan-a-Mural machine, a kind of robotic device that automatically copies an image using computer-controlled jets of paint. In *Figure*, 1990 *(illus. p. 83)*, a cowboy's head, half in shadow and looking as if it were a negative image, floats above the ruffled collar of the body of a headless clown.

More recently Nechvatal has begun to work with computer viruses, the bits of digital code that can destroy software programs and computer disks and are often capable of replicating themselves to infect other systems. Working at a computer laboratory in Arbois, France, Nechvatal has loaded his images into a powerful computer and infected them with viruses he created in conjunction with a programmer.

Kunie Sugiura

Born in Japan, Kunie Sugiura studied at the Art Institute of Chicago and now lives in New York. A painter as well as a photographer, she began to produce photograms in the early 1980s by making graffitilike marks on canvases coated with photoemulsion. In recent years she has used natural objects, including squid, catfish, flowers, and cats, as elements in her photograms. For a recent series of works she placed kittens on large pieces of photosensitized paper. The finished pieces record not only the kittens' movements around the paper but also the stains left by their urine.

In *Rose Veins–2*, 1990 *(illus. p. 79)*, Sugiura has arranged a bouquet of roses in a spiral on the photographic sheet. With its pale color, mottled background, and sunburst shape, the picture seems to trace a pattern of floral contrails in a cloudy sky, as if an unlikely aerobatic troupe were performing high above the ground.

Anita Douthat

As a graduate student at the University of New Mexico in the early 1980s, Anita Douthat wrote a critical and historical investigation of the photogram. For her the photogram process provides a way of creating what she calls a "semi-abstract, symbolic language" and of "transforming the impressions of ordinary objects into mysterious presences."

Douthat creates images in which simple but powerful forms are combined with striking effects of light and color. Her images are often taken from scientific sources and reflect her interest in natural history as well as expressing the emotional impact of events in her life.

Of the work created between 1989 and 1991 *(illus. p. 82)*, which was begun after she was injured in an accident and a family member died, Douthat writes that it took on a new significance for her, "that of expressing fragility and the presence of absence."

Floris M. Neusüss

Born in 1937, the German photographer Floris M. Neusüss has been making photograms since 1960. As head of the photography program at the Hochshule für Bildende Kunste in Kassel since

1971, Neusüss has been an energetic advocate for photograms—teaching, organizing exhibitions, and writing an important history of the process.

Many of Neusüss's own works record the body as a dematerialized, shadowy form *(illus. p. 70)*. Often larger than life-sized, displaying great command of the photogram process, and incorporating images of flowers, plants, and other elements, these pieces make use of the seemingly primal quality of photograms, their apparent closeness to the forces of nature.

Susan Rankaitis

In the large photograms she has made over the past half-dozen years, Susan Rankaitis has focused on issues of science and technology and addressed such topics as chaos theory, supercolliders, and chromosomes. In *G,* 1992 *(illus. p. 86)*, she considers the structure of DNA; the piece is one of a series of four based on the letters *A, C, G,* and *T,* the common abbreviations for the base nucleotides that make up the spiraling chains of DNA molecules. Shaped like the letter *G,* the photogram also includes negative images of representations of DNA molecules.

But the form of the work is as important as its content. A former painter, Rankaitis stains and paints her photograms with photographic chemicals to produce subtle colors and varying tones of light and dark. She began the DNA series in an effort to understand how individuality is built up out of such a small number of repeated elements.

Philip Pocock

To create his abstract images, Philip Pocock paints Cibachrome photographic paper with various chemical solutions as if it were canvas. With their iridescent colors and ambiguous space, the resulting works combine the suggestiveness of abstract painting with the impersonal, manufactured look of photographs *(illus. p. 85)*.

In making his works in this manner Pocock carries out his belief in the importance of the photograph as an object rather than a description of the world. "What Minor White called the 'essence' of a photograph," Pocock wrote in a recent letter, "is not in my view reflected in the skin of the subject, but the skin of the photograph itself. The world and its subjects for me just get between the viewer and the nature of the medium."

Whether to get at the essence of photography or of the world, the photogram continues to provide contemporary artists with a valuable tool of expression and analysis. The diversity and strength of the work included here suggest how capable and flexible a tool the process can be.

**ROBERT
RAUSCHENBERG
AND
SUSAN WEIL**

From top:

Fugue
1951
10 ⅛ x 5½ in.

*Suspended Shadow
Declared Eternal by
the Death of Time*
1951
9 ⅞ x 5 ⅝ in.

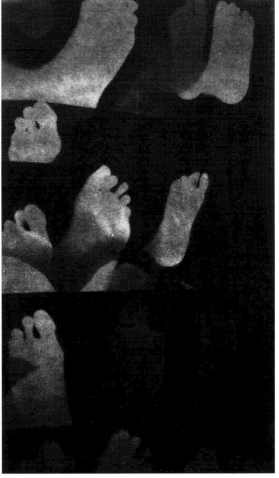

Smoke on Glass
1963
13¼ x 10⅜ in.

Skull & Milky Way
1966
28 7/8 x 24 3/4 x 3 1/2 in.

New Angel
1974
85 x 39 in.

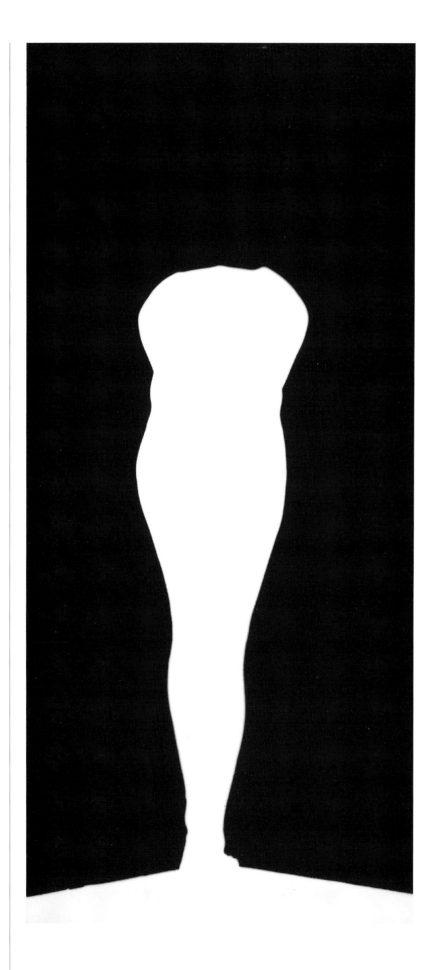

Language of Echoes
1987
42½ x 36¾ in.

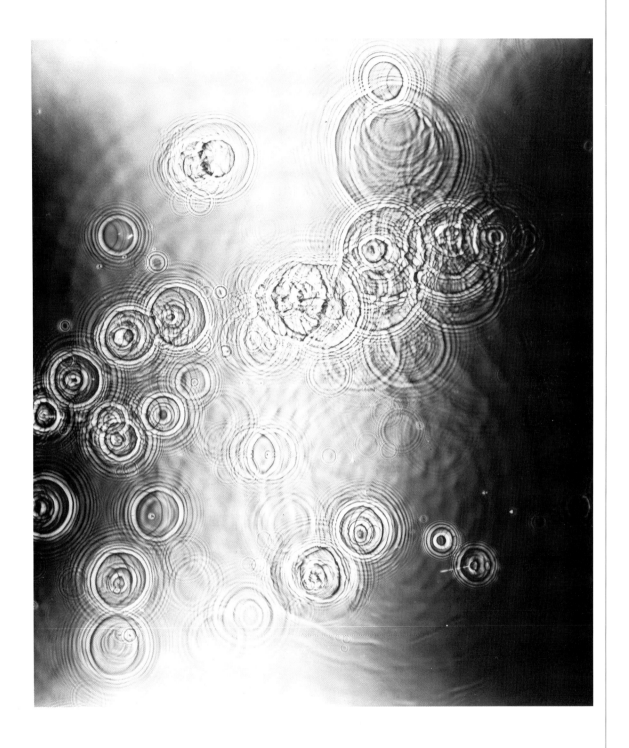

FLORIS NEUSUSS

Photogram
1991
98 x 42 in.

ROBERT HEINECKEN

Are You Rea? #9-6
1966
10¼ x 8⅞ in.

Are You Rea? #10-3
1966
11¾ x 9 in.

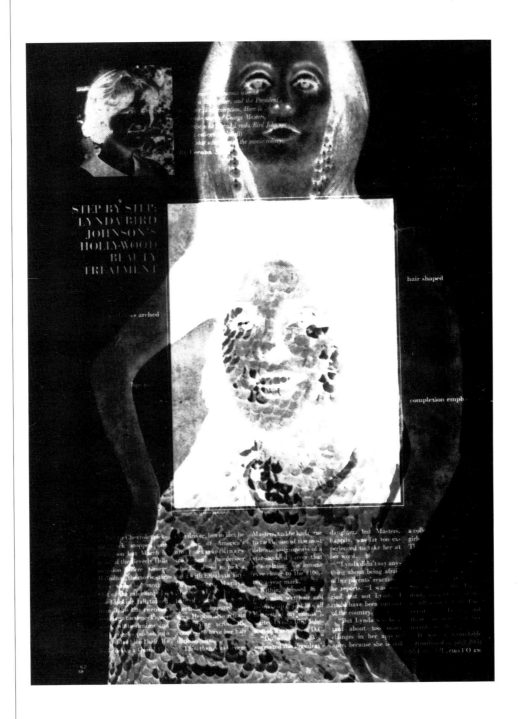

Fast Food / Pasta Salad
1983
22½ x 30½ in.

ROBERT HEINECKEN

Fast Food / Chili Dog
1983
22 x 30½ in.

Untitled 76/17
1976
30 x 40 in.

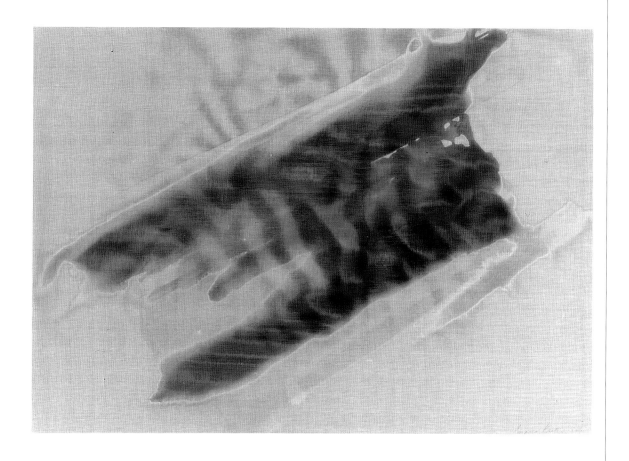

Artificial Curiosities
1984
24 x 31⅜ in.

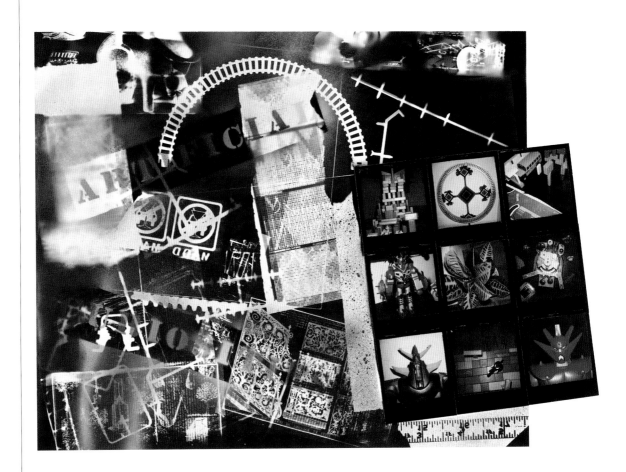

SIGMAR POLKE

Der Jungbrunnen
(The Fountain
of Youth)
1984
50 x 82 in.

Hand/Snake
1987
40 x 30 x 2 in.

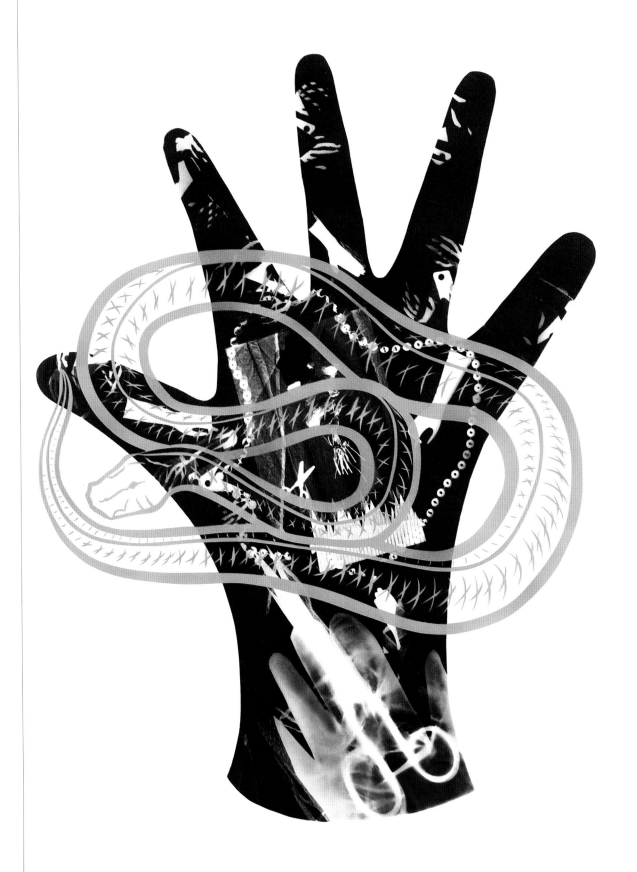

Rose Veins–2
1990
41 x 31 ½ in.

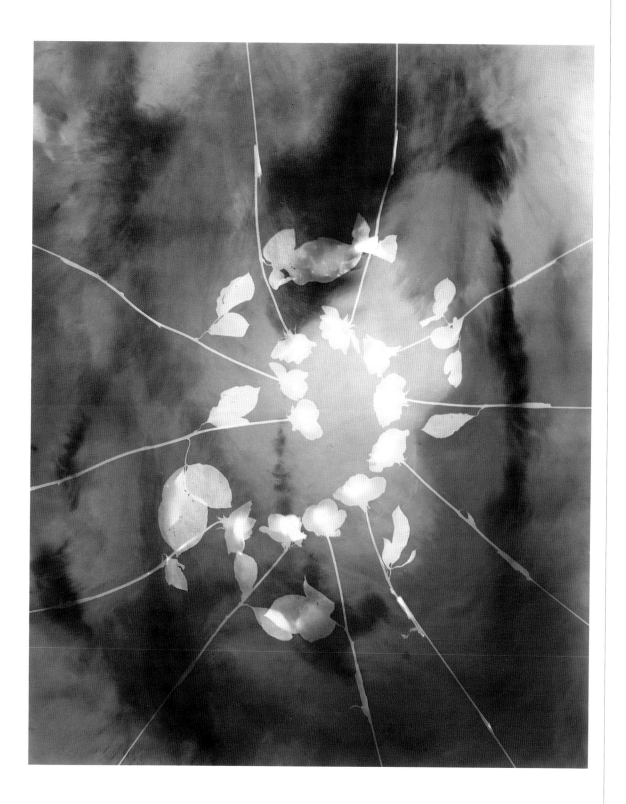

IRTS
1989
24 x 20 in.

Funnel Series
1990
24 x 20 in.

Figure
1990
76 x 38 in.

Untitled
1992
57½ × 40½ in.

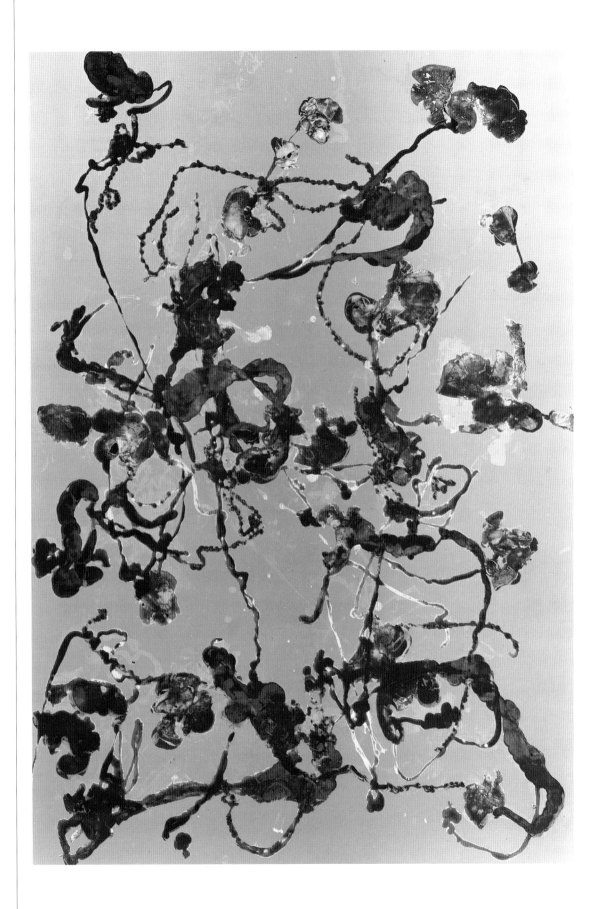

SUSAN RANKAITIS

G
1992
75 x 50 in.

WORKS IN THE EXHIBITION

All measurements give height before width.

THOMAS BARROW
American (b. 1938)
Artificial Curiosities, 1984, gelatin silver print with spray lacquers and attached SX-70 Polaroids, 24 x 31 3/8 in.
Courtesy Andrew Smith Gallery, Santa Fe. Illus. p. 76.

ELIZABETH R. BRYANT
American (b. 1961)
Hand/Snake, 1987, black and white photogram with enamel, 40 x 30 x 2 in. Collection of the artist. Illus. p. 78.

BRUCE CONNER
American (b. 1933)
New Angel, 1974, photogram, 85 x 39 in. Courtesy Fraenkel Gallery, San Francisco. Illus. p. 68.

ANITA DOUTHAT
American (b. 1950)
Funnel Series, 1990, photogram, 24 x 20 in. Courtesy of the artist and Benteler-Morgan Galleries, Houston. Illus. p. 82.

ADAM FUSS
English (b. 1961)
Language of Echoes, 1987, photogram, 42 1/2 x 36 3/4 in. Denver Art Museum: Joyce R. Strauss Fund. Illus. p. 69.

Untitled, 1992, Cibachrome photogram, 57 1/2 x 40 1/2 in. Private collection. Illus. p. 84.

GILBERT & GEORGE
Gilbert, Italian (b. 1943)
George, English (b. 1942)
Raining Gin, 1973, photogram, 78 x 45 in. Courtesy Sonnabend Gallery. Illus. p. 67.

RAOUL HAUSMANN
Austrian (1886-1971)
Untitled, 1948, montage-photograph on photogram, 13 3/4 x 11 in. Musée Départemental de Rochechouart (87) France. Photo: Freddy le Soux. Illus. p. 34.

Untitled, 1950, gelatin silver print, 13 7/8 x 11 1/4 in. Museum Folkwang, Essen, Germany. Illus. p. 35.

Untitled, 1951, photogram, 15 3/4 x 11 7/8 in. Musée Départemental de Rochechouart (87) France. Illus. p. 36.

Untitled, 1954, photopictogram, 15 5/16 x 11 7/8 in. Musée Départemental de Rochechouart (87) France. Illus. p. 37.

ROBERT HEINECKEN
American (b. 1931)
Are You Rea? #9-6, 1966, photogram, 10 1/4 x 8 7/8 in. Courtesy Pace/Macgill Gallery, New York. © Robert Heinecken. Illus. p. 71.

Are You Rea? #10-3, 1966, photogram, 11 3/4 x 9 in. Courtesy Pace/Macgill Gallery, New York. © Robert Heinecken. Illus. p. 72.

Fast Food / Pasta Salad, 1983, photogram, Polaroid color print, 22 1/2 x 30 1/2 in. Museum of Photographic Arts, San Diego. Illus. p. 73.

Fast Food / Chili Dog, 1983, photogram, Polaroid color print, 22 x 30 1/2 in. Museum of Photographic Arts, San Diego. Illus. p. 74.

BARBARA KASTEN
American (b. 1936)
Untitled 76/17, 1976, photogenic painting with mixed non-silver emulsions and inks, 30 x 40 in. Courtesy John Weber Gallery, New York. Illus. p. 75.

GYORGY KEPES
American (b. Hungary, 1906)
Untitled, c. 1937-39, photogram, photograph with hand-colored drawing, 11 7/16 x 8 7/8 in. Private collection. Illus. p. 48.

Photogram, 1977, gelatin silver print, 20 x 16 in. Private collection. Illus. p. 49.

MAN RAY
American (1890-1976)
Untitled (Rayograph), 1922, gelatin silver print, 11 7/16 x 9 5/16 in. The Museum of Modern Art, New York: Gift of James Thrall Soby. © 1993 ARS, New York/ADAGP and the Man Ray Trust, Paris. Illus. p. 17.

Untitled (Rayograph), 1923, gelatin silver print, 9 7/16 x 7 1/8 in. The Museum of Modern Art, New York: Gift of James Thrall Soby. © 1993 ARS, New York/ADAGP and the Man Ray Trust, Paris. Illus. p. 18.

The Spiral, 1923, rayograph, 11 3/16 x 9 3/8 in. Yale University Art Gallery: Gift of Collection Société Anonyme. © 1993 ARS, New York/ADAGP and the Man Ray Trust, Paris. Illus. p. 19.

Gun with Alphabet Squares, 1924, rayograph, gelatin silver print, 11 5/8 x 9 1/4 in. The J. Paul Getty Museum, Malibu. © 1993 ARS, New York/ADAGP and the Man Ray Trust, Paris. Illus. p. 20.

Hand and Flower, 1925, rayograph, gelatin silver print, 11 9/16 x 9 1/4 in. The J. Paul Getty Museum, Malibu. © 1993 ARS, New York/ADAGP and the Man Ray Trust, Paris. Illus. p. 21.

Sugar Loaves, 1925, rayograph, 9 3/16 x 11 5/8 in. Yale University Art Gallery: Gift of Collection Société Anonyme. © 1993 ARS, New York/ADAGP and the Man Ray Trust, Paris. Illus. p. 22.

Clock Wheels, 1925, rayograph, 11 x 9 in. Yale University Art Gallery: Gift of Collection Société Anonyme. © 1993 ARS, New York/ADAGP and the Man Ray Trust, Paris. Illus. p. 23.

Abstraction–Lines, 1928, rayograph, gelatin silver print, 14 7/8 x 11 1/16 in. The J. Paul Getty Museum, Malibu. © 1993 ARS, New York/ADAGP and the Man Ray Trust, Paris. Illus. p. 24.

Untitled, 1943, rayograph, 13 15/16 x 10 15/16 in. Denver Art Museum: Gift of Mr. and Mrs. Walter Maitland. © 1993 ARS, New York/ADAGP and the Man Ray Trust, Paris. Illus. p. 25.

LASZLO MOHOLY-NAGY
American (b. Hungary, 1895-1946)
Untitled, 1922, photogram, gelatin silver print, 3 1/2 x 5 1/2 in. Collection of Robert Shapazian, Los Angeles. Illus. p. 26.

Untitled (Goerz), 1925, photogram, gelatin silver print, 11 7/8 x 8 7/8 in. George Eastman House. Illus. p. 28.

Untitled (Goerz), 1925, photogram, gelatin silver print, 11 7/8 x 8 7/8 in. George Eastman House. Illus. p. 29.

Self-Portrait, 1925, photogram, gelatin silver print, 15 5/8 x 11 5/8 in. George Eastman House. Illus. p. 31.

Blumenfotogramm, 1925, gelatin silver print, 9 5/16 x 7 in. Berlinische Galerie Photographische Sammlung. Illus. p. 30.

Hand Photogram, c. 1925, gelatin silver print, 9 3/8 x 7 1/16 in. Los Angeles County Museum of Art: Ralph M. Parson Fund. Illus. p. 27.

Untitled, 1925, photogram, gelatin silver print, 7 1/8 x 9 7/16 in. Collection Robert Shapazian, Los Angeles. Illus. p. 32.

Untitled, c. 1939, photogram, gelatin silver print, 20 1/4 x 16 in. Collection of Jerry and Emily Spiegel. Photo: Zidman/Fremont. Illus. p. 33.

JOSEPH NECHVATAL
American (b. 1951)
Figure, 1990, acrylic on canvas, computer/robotic assisted, 76 x 38 in. Courtesy Brooke Alexander, New York. Illus. p. 83.

FLORIS NEUSUSS
German (b. 1937)
Photogram, 1991, gelatin silver print, 98 x 42 in. Courtesy of the artist and Benteler-Morgan Galleries, Houston. Illus. p. 70.

PHILIP POCOCK
Canadian (b. 1954)
Thinking about Utopia, 1992, Cibachrome, 24 x 20 1/8 in. Courtesy of the artist. Illus. p. 85.

SIGMAR POLKE
Polish (b. 1941)
Der Jungbrunnen (The Fountain of Youth), 1984, toned gelatin silver print, 50 x 82 in. Los Angeles County Museum of Art: Purchased with funds provided by the Art Museum Council, 1992. Illus. p. 77.

SUSAN RANKAITIS
American (b. 1949)
G, 1992, photogram, mixed media on paper, 75 x 50 in. Courtesy of the artist and Ruth Bloom Gallery, Santa Monica. Illus. p. 86.

ROBERT RAUSCHENBERG
American (b. 1925)
SUSAN WEIL
American (b. 1930)
Untitled, 1951, photograph of original blueprint c. 1949, 12 x 7 1/8 in. Private collection. Photo: George Hixson, Houston. Illus. p. 63.

Fugue, 1951, photograph of original blueprint c. 1949, 10 1/8 x 5 1/2 in. Private collection. Photo: George Hixson, Houston. Illus. p. 64.

Suspended Shadow Declared Eternal by the Death of Time, 1951, photograph of original blueprint c. 1949, 9 7/8 x 5 5/8 in. Private collection. Photo: George Hixson, Houston. Illus. p. 64.

THEODORE ROSZAK
American (b. Poland, 1907-1981)
Untitled, 1937-41, photogram, gelatin silver print, 4 3/4 x 4 in. Courtesy Hirschl & Adler Galleries, New York. Photo: Helga Photo Studio. Illus. p. 50.

Untitled, 1937-41, photogram, gelatin silver print, 10 x 8 in. Courtesy Hirschl & Adler Galleries, New York. Photo: Helga Photo Studio. Illus. p. 51.

LUCAS SAMARAS
American (b. Greece, 1936)
Skull & Milky Way, 1966, X-ray and photograph with pins, 28 7/8 x 24 3/4 x 3 1/2 in. Whitney Museum of American Art: Gift of Howard and Jean Lipman 91.34.6. Photo: Gregory Clements. Illus. p. 66.

CHRISTIAN SCHAD
German (1894-1982)
Untitled Schadograph, 1919, gelatin silver printing-out paper, 2 3/8 x 2 25/32 in. The J. Paul Getty Museum, Malibu. Illus. p. 15.

Schadograph, 1919, printing-out paper, 3 1/8 x 2 3/8 in. The Museum of Fine Arts, Houston: Museum purchase with funds provided by Isabell and Max Herzstein. Photo: A. Newbourn. Illus. p. 15.

Amourette, 1919, gelatin silver print, 2 1/2 x 3 1/2 in. The Museum of Modern Art, New York: Purchase. Illus. p. 16.

Renseignements, 1919, schadograph, 2 5/16 x 3 5/16 in. Quillan Company, courtesy Jill Quasha. Illus. p. 16.

Transmission Ischiatique, 1919, schadograph, 2 3/8 x 3 1/4 in., Gilman Paper Company. Illus. p. 16.

ARTHUR SIEGEL
American (1913-1978)
Photogram, c. 1940, gelatin silver print, 14 x 11 in. Courtesy Simon Lowinsky Gallery, New York. Illus. p. 45.

Lucidagram, 1967, gelatin silver print, 17 x 14 in. Courtesy Simon Lowinsky Gallery, New York. Not illustrated.

Lucidagram, 1969, gelatin silver print, 17 x 14 in. Courtesy Simon Lowinsky Gallery, New York. Not illustrated.

Lucidagram, 1970, gelatin silver print, 17 x 14 in. Courtesy Simon Lowinsky Gallery, New York. Illus. p. 46.

Lucidagram, c. 1970, gelatin silver print, 14 x 17 in. Courtesy Simon Lowinsky Gallery, New York. Illus. p. 47.

HENRY HOLMES SMITH
American (1909-1986)
#3 Refraction Drawing, c. 1949, refraction print, 13 7/8 x 10 7/8 in. Courtesy Smith Family Trust and the Howard Greenberg Gallery. Illus. p. 52.

#2 Untitled, 1950, refraction print, 10 7/8 x 13 7/8 in. Courtesy Smith Family Trust and the Howard Greenberg Gallery. Illus. p. 53.

FREDERICK SOMMER
American (b. Italy, 1905)
Smoke on Glass, 1963, photogram, 13 1/4 x 10 3/8 in. Private collection. Illus. p. 65.

KUNIE SUGIURA
Japanese (b. 1942)
Rose Veins–2, 1990, photogram, gelatin silver print on aluminum, 41 x 31 1/2 in. Collection of the artist. Photo: D. James Dee. Illus. p. 79.

JAMES WELLING
American (b. 1951)
IRTS, 1989, photogram, Polaroid color print, 24 x 20 in. Courtesy Jay Gorney Modern Art, New York. Illus. p. 80.

IRBX, 1989, photogram, Polaroid color print, 24 x 20 in. Courtesy Jay Gorney Modern Art, New York. Illus. p. 81.